Mao Zedong

A Captivating Guide to the Life of a Chairman of the Communist Party of China, the Cultural Revolution and the Political Theory of Maoism

© Copyright 2018

All Rights Reserved. No part of this book may be reproduced in any form without permission in writing from the author. Reviewers may quote brief passages in reviews.

Disclaimer: No part of this publication may be reproduced or transmitted in any form or by any means, mechanical or electronic, including photocopying or recording, or by any information storage and retrieval system, or transmitted by email without permission in writing from the publisher.

While all attempts have been made to verify the information provided in this publication, neither the author nor the publisher assumes any responsibility for errors, omissions or contrary interpretations of the subject matter herein.

This book is for entertainment purposes only. The views expressed are those of the author alone and should not be taken as expert instruction or commands. The reader is responsible for his or her own actions.

Adherence to all applicable laws and regulations, including international, federal, state and local laws governing professional licensing, business practices, advertising and all other aspects of doing business in the US, Canada, UK or any other jurisdiction is the sole responsibility of the purchaser or reader.

Neither the author nor the publisher assumes any responsibility or liability whatsoever on behalf of the purchaser or reader of these materials. Any perceived slight of any individual or organization is purely unintentional.

Free Bonus from Captivating History (Available for a Limited time)

Hi History Lovers!

Now you have a chance to join our exclusive history list so you can get your first history ebook for free as well as discounts and a potential to get more history books for free! Simply visit the link below to join.

Captivatinghistory.com/ebook

Also, make sure to follow us on:
Twitter: @Captivhistory
Facebook: Captivating History:@captivatinghistory

Contents

INTRODUCTION 1

CHAPTER 1 – EARLY LIFE 4

CHAPTER 2 – POLITICAL AWAKENINGS 9

CHAPTER 3 – BEIJING 16

CHAPTER 4 – MAY FOURTH AND THE NEW CULTURE MOVEMENT 19

CHAPTER 5 – THE COMMUNIST PARTY OF CHINA'S GROWING PAINS 28

CHAPTER 6 – THE NORTHERN EXPEDITION 36

CHAPTER 7 – COMMUNISTS AT LARGE 40

CHAPTER 8 – THE LONG MARCH 44

CHAPTER 9 – THE PEOPLE'S REPUBLIC OF CHINA 46

CHAPTER 10 – THE GREAT LEAP FORWARD 50

CHAPTER 11 – THE CULTURAL REVOLUTION 54

CHAPTER 12 – WHAT DID MAOISM STAND FOR? 58

CONCLUSION 60

PRIMARY AND SECONDARY SOURCES 83

Introduction

Mao Zedong – was known as "Chairman Mao" to millions of Chinese citizens – is recognized alongside Chiang Kai-Shek and Sun Yat-Sen as one of the most influential figures of modern Chinese history. His political control of the nation waned during his later years, but he remained the Chairman of the Communist Party of China since it was established in 1949 to the day he died (September 9, 1976). As the founding father of the People's Republic of China and the centerpiece of one of the world's most intense personality cults, the extent of his influence is difficult to understate[i].

Mao was not just a communist revolutionary or a political leader. He was also a poet, a political theorist, and a brilliant orator. His similarly influential successor Deng Xiaoping[ii], who served as the de facto leader of the People's Republic of China from 1978 until his retirement in 1989, is acknowledged worldwide for steering the nation towards economic growth. His legacy can be judged by the physical markers of economic development: infrastructure in the form of roads, highways, buildings, factories, skyscrapers, cities, gross domestic output, etc.

While Mao is credited for catalyzing China's transition from a mostly agrarian nation into a modern industrial powerhouse, his legacy cannot be confined to economics alone. Deng's pragmatism and emphasis on individual self-interest may prevail in contemporary China, but Mao still inspires widespread devotion. Some prominent pictures and statues of Mao in the country have been quietly removed, but his portrait still figures prominently in Beijing's Tiananmen Square. He joins the ranks of some of the world's most famous community cult-of-personality leaders in having his corpse being on public display: Russia's Vladimir Lenin, Vietnam's Ho Chi Minh and North Korea's Kim Il Sung and Kim Jong-il. His embalmed corpse lies in a crystal cabinet within a stately Soviet-inspired memorial hall in the middle of Tiananmen Square, attracting long lines of visitors.

His legacy as a political leader is marked by significant successes and catastrophic failures – a historical reality that remains controversial in contemporary China's censor-prone, one-party state. His contributions to the nation as a political genius and ideological visionary – raising its average life expectancy, championing gender equality, improving popular literacy, promoting the collectivization of agriculture, ensuring accessibility to medical services, ushering in a period of unity and stability after decades of civil war and foreign invasion, restoring its sense of pride, dignity and confidence after a "Century of Humiliation" and positioning it towards the world economic and military power it is today – were magnified and glorified during his reign.

His theories, clever military strategies, and political policies (which are collectively known as Maoism) inspired anti-capitalism and anti-imperialist sentiments. Mao's charisma and force of personality gained him widespread approval, respect, admiration, and devotion in his home country. He was also able to charm Western intellectuals and political leaders like the American journalist Robert Snow (who wrote his first biography), Harvard professor John K. Fairbank, feminist philosopher Simone de Beauvoir, and French philosopher Jean-Paul Sartre[iii].

Mao's image as a benevolent protector of the people and his humble origins from the peasant class made it easier to suppress the brutal realities of his authoritarian rule. His grandiose ambitions for China to become a military superpower lead to a disastrous nation-wide diversion from agriculture to industrial arms-making. As a result, an estimated 45 million people starved to death during The Great Famine from 1958 to 1961. Historian R. J. Rummel has pointed out that all the major global wars from 1900 – 1987 – World War I, World War II, the Vietnam War, the Korean War, and the Mexican and Russian Revolutions – amounted to a death count of over 34 million people[iv].

Under his Cultural Revolution (1966 – 1976), Chinese culture and intellectual life suffered tremendously. Chinese classics of literature, poetry, and philosophy were burned across the nation. Foreign works of art, literature, and culture were banned for being "counterrevolutionary." Respected artisans and intellectuals were stripped of their respect, dignity, and professions.

Today, Mao's legacy can inspire slavish devotion, outright condemnation, as well as a hesitance to look too closely at the negative aspects of his legacy. The fact that his influence spanned over nearly three decades also makes it difficult to arrive at a holistic understanding of his impact on China. The official line from the Community Party of China, which was popularized by Deng Xiaoping, is that Mao was "70 percent correct and 30 percent wrong"[v]. This biography will detail Mao's remarkable journey, from being the son of a peasant to one of modern history's greatest – and highly polarizing – leaders. It aims to provide a better understanding of Mao as a person and to try to unpack the personality traits and personal experiences that shaped his worldview and actions.

Chapter 1 – Early Life

Mao was not born into political or intellectual privilege, but he was not born into poverty either. He was born on December 26, 1893, in the remote village of Shaoshan in the Hunan province. His father, Mao Yi-chang, was unlike the average Chinese peasant who toiled in poverty. Despite only possessing two years of formal schooling, he had improved his status and wealth through hard work, frugality, and shrewdness[vi]. As a rich grain dealer and land-owning farmer, he expected his son to gain knowledge of the Confucian classics, accounting and bookkeeping, and to contribute to his business when he became older. To him, the pursuit of knowledge was for purely utilitarian ends. Mao would recount one of his father's favorite sayings to his daughter Li Min: "Poverty is not the result of eating too much or spending too much. Poverty comes from an inability to do sums. Whoever can do sums will have enough to live by; whoever cannot will squander even mountains of gold![vii]"

His father was stern, authoritative, and prone to violent bursts of temper. Despite being the eldest son (he was technically the third-born son, but his two older brothers had died in infancy), Mao was not spared from harsh beatings by his father. His two younger brothers Mao Zemin and Mao Zetan and his adopted younger sister Mao Zejian were also beaten. Mao and his siblings found refuge and comfort in his gentle mother Wen Qimei, who was a devout Buddhist. She tried to share her religious outlook with her son and often brought him to the nearby Buddhist temple to pray. She hoped he might decide to become a monk and would promote peace as he followed in the Buddha's footsteps.

Mao would fulfill neither of his parents' ambitions for him. With his exceptional memory, he easily mastered the Confucian principles that his father had sent him to learn in elementary school. He was nevertheless personally uninspired by Confucius' emphasis on moral perfection and filial piety. Instead of adhering to Confucius' commandment that children obey their parents and elders, Mao openly contradicted and opposed his father and teachers (and strategically used Confucian quotations to support his position). His biographers Jung Chang and her husband John Halliday noted that he would argue that his father, being the older individual, should perform more manual labor than him, a younger child. They point out that this was "an unthinkably insolent argument by Chinese standards," which certainly did not elevate individual conscience over paternal authority.

From a young age, Mao demonstrated an unconventional and highly atypical (given the cultural context) to assert his own will and to defy traditional authority. He was also able to use his intelligence to manipulate his adversaries. In their biography, Chang and Halliday describe how his argument with his father (in front of several guests) played out:

"My father scolded me before them, calling me lazy and useless. This infuriated me. I called him names and left the house … My father … pursued me, cursing me as well as commanding me to come back. I reached the edge of a pond and threatened to jump in if he came any nearer … My father backed down […] Old men like him didn't want to lose their sons. This is their weakness. I attacked at their weak point, and I won![viii]"

When he was 13, he could no longer tolerate his teacher's reliance on physical abuse as a pedagogical tool. Contented with the amount of learning he had amassed thus far, his father happily arranged for him to begin working full-time on the family farm. (He had been assigned various farming tasks by the time he was six years old). However, Mao was not personally interested in his father's commercial pursuits, Confucius' humanism, or his mother's religious outlook as a child.

Instead, he was passionately devoted to Chinese historical literature that described heroic uprisings, upheavals, and revolutions. He ardently consumed narratives of adventurers, warriors, knights, and fighters in texts such as *The Biography of the Ever-Faithful Yue Fei, Water Margin, The Three Kingdoms, Journey to the West* and *The Romance of Sui and Tang*. He kept his reading habit hidden from his father, who would become outraged at the sight of such as "useless" pursuit. When he came across Zhen Guanying's *Words of Warning to an Affluent Age* (1893), he began to develop an interest in the politics of the era. Zheng's book presented a vision of how to modernize China by deserting its traditional Confucian order and establishing a British-type constitutional monarchy.

While Mao was broadening his intellectual horizons, his parents were making plans for his future without his consent. By the time he learnt of their plan to marry him (at 14) to Luo Yigu, the daughter of a rural intellectual who was four years older than him, his marriage contract to her had been signed. (Mao Yichang himself had been married at 15). The wedding date had been agreed on, and his father had sent the customary gifts and bride-price to his soon-to-be father-in-law Luo Helou. Mao revealed to his first biographer John Snow that he had not consummated the marriage[ix]. Not long after his wedding, he deserted his parents, family, and wife to live in the house of an unemployed student in Shaoshan. Luo Yigu would quietly endure the humiliation of being described as "neither a married woman nor a maiden" for two years, before dying of dysentery shortly after her twentieth birthday on February 11, 1910[x].

Free from the demands of his parents and responsibilities on the farm, Mao could focus solely on his reading. During this formative time, he explored nonfiction historical and political texts. He digested older texts like *Records of the Grand Historian* by ancient Chinese historian

Sima Qian and Ban Gu's *History of the Former Han Dynasty*. He also read texts that explored China's contemporary struggles with foreign aggressors and invaders, such as Feng Guifen's *Personal Protests from the Study of Jiao Bin* (1861)[xi]. After reading a pamphlet written by young Chinese revolutionary Chen Tianhua, he developed an acute understanding of the losses and humiliation that China had suffered at the hands of Japan and Britain.

When Mao eventually reached out to his father to ask for financial assistance to pursue his education when he was 16, he decided to forgive his "ungrateful son." Mao enrolled in Dongshan Higher Primary School, which was located approximately 15 miles away from Shaoshan. There, Mao would be exposed to contemporary subjects such as physics, chemistry, and biology. This was the first time Mao ventured beyond the cloistered confines of his native village.

Mao may have had grand ambitions for himself in his head, but his classmates fixated on his provincial origins. At his new school, Mao's peers were the arrogant sons of wealthy landlords from the neighboring Xiangxiang district. They disapproved of his regional dialect and lack of an impressive wardrobe. Mao made very few friends and suffered under the hostility he received from the majority of his peers.

Instead of keeping a low profile, he was determined to succeed. He endured the insults and eventually impressed his teachers with his intelligence and capacity for hard work. His education provided further exposure to the various rulers that attained glory in China's illustrious past: Yao and Shun, Qin Shi Huangdi, and Wu Di. He also gained exposure to foreign history and developed an admiration for the military and political acumen of Western historical icons like Napoleon, George Washington, Catherine the Great, and Abraham Lincoln[xii].

He was particularly inspired when he learnt of Japan's victory over Russia in 1905. The victory was symbolic on two fronts. On the one hand, it was a triumph of an Asian country over an intimidating European power via the embrace of political modernization. On the other, it was a victory of a constitutional monarchy over despotism. The idea of China emerging from the backwaters and pursuing a path to similar eminence on a global scale was within his consciousness as he decided to leave Dongshan School for a middle school in Changsha: the capital city of the Hunan province.

Chapter 2 – Political Awakenings

Changsha was over three thousand years old and had recently been the primary base for the suppression of the Taiping Rebellion[xiii]. It opened to foreign trade in 1904. When Mao arrived at his first city in early 1911, he experienced the wonders of cosmopolitanism. Changsha was home to a few Western schools, including a missionary medical college. Mao was awed by the sight of electric lights, stone-paved streets, and the city's towering stone wall. He was most amazed, however, by the sight of the railroad (that had been constructed three years earlier) and the locomotive train. There were a small number of foreigners in the city, mainly the Americans who had established a Yale University branch and a hospital there.

Mao was pleasantly surprised he had gained admission to a vaunted school in the city. Here, he was exposed to new theories and ideas from the West through the works of reformers such as Liang Qichao and Sun Yat-sen[xiv]. One could argue, however, that his "real education" occurred through the six months he spent as a soldier. On October 10, 1911, an anti-monarchical uprising against the Qing dynasty began in Wuchang, the capital of Hubei Province. Many soldiers from the Eighth Engineer Battalion of the New Army there were members of the revolutionary Progressive Society, which were closely linked to the Revolutionary Alliance led by Sun Yat-Sen. They quickly gained control of the entire city and sparked a wave of anti-Manchu uprisings in neighboring cities. Within just two weeks, the rebellion had spread to Changsha. When November ended, fifteen out of China's eighteen provinces had defected from Qing authority.

News of these transformative events galvanized Mao's evolution from a patriotic supporter of the Chinese monarchy to an anti-monarchical revolutionary. Even before he received news of the Wuchang uprising, he had decided to cut off the long pigtail that all Chinese men were required to wear as a sign of submission and loyalty to the Manchus. As the conflict between the revolutionaries and Qing monarchy escalated, Mao decided to join the revolutionary Hunan army as it made plans to invade the north.

On December 25, Sun Yat-Sen returned to China. Instead of negotiating with the prime minister appointed by the Qing court (Yuan Shikai), Sun prepared for a military confrontation. He proclaimed the founding of the Republic of China in Nanjing on January 1, 1912 as the president of the National Assembly (which was composed by delegates from the 15 rebellious provinces)[xv]. There was to be, however, no major military conflict. Most of the National Assembly delegates wanted the monarchy to be dissolved, but they did not want a revolutionary like Sun Yat-Sen to assume control of the newly-formed republic. After China's last emperor – the six-year-old Pu Yi – abdicated the throne on February 12, 1912, Sun Yat-Sen resigned from his position as Yuan Shikai was elected the provisional president of the Republic of China.

Mao did not experience significant military action during the six months he spent as a soldier. He nevertheless obtained a first-hand experience of military life – a realization of his fascination with the famed military strategists of history. As a soldier, Mao was paid a relatively high salary of seven silver dollars each month. He would reveal to Edgar Snow, however, that he saw himself as a class apart from most of his fellow soldiers, who were illiterate and poor (and thus joined the army for food)[xvi]. Instead of carrying water from outside the city like his comrades, he decided to buy it.

After Mao was discharged from the military, he explored his choices. He certainly did not have a clear idea of what he wanted. He first decided to enroll in police school, and then decided to try his hand at soap making. After that, he pursued law school, a commercial middle school, and then a higher commercial public school. In the spring of 1912, he decided to enroll at Hunan Higher Provincial School. Rather than sticking to the prescribed curriculum, however, he pursued independent learning at the Hunan provincial library. There, he studied the classic texts of the Western liberal tradition alongside collections of foreign history, Greek myths, and international geography. At 19, he had his first encounter with a world map. He also gained a foothold in political activity by helping to establish a number of student organizations. This included the New People's Study Society (est. 1917-18). Several members of this society would eventually join the Communist Party.

Angered by his lack of direction and numerous changes of plans, his father compelled him to enroll in a professional program (or else proceed without his financial assistance). Despite his humble origins, Mao considered himself to be an intellectual, i.e. a class above the peasants, coolies, and soldiers who were required to contribute manual labor[xvii]. The revolution may have occurred, but the vast majority of Chinese citizens at the time were still illiterate and working as construction workers, coolies, peddlers, and porters. Unwilling to pursue manual labor or earn his living as a tutor, he decided to heed his father's wishes. In 1913, he enrolled at the Hunan Provincial Fourth Normal School with plans to become a teacher. In March 1914, the local authorities decided to merge the school with the more reputable and larger Provincial First Normal School.

The First Normal School was relatively new, having been founded in 1903 – towards the last years of the Qing dynasty. The people of Changsha referred to it as the "Western palace" because of its European architecture, and the teachers Mao encountered there embodied its structural modernism[xviii]. They had been educated overseas and were well-versed in French, Japanese and English. A few of them would exert a significant influence on the young Mao. Yuan

Jiliu taught him to write impressive essays, while Xu Teli and Fang Weixia (who were both members of the Revolutionary Alliance and had participated in the 1911 Revolution) solidified Mao's patriotism and his faith in the idea of China being governed as a republic.

The educator that Mao held in the highest regard was Yang Changji, the head of the school's philosophy department and a devoted fitness enthusiast. Yang had studied in Japan, Germany, and Scotland, and could easily impress his students with his formidable knowledge of both Chinese and Western ethics and philosophy. He also taught logic and pedagogy and subscribed to Western liberalism – which he saw as equivalent to the philosophies of Confucian thinkers Wang Yangming and Wang Chuanshan. Mao recounted his admiration for Yang to his friend: "When I think of [his] greatness, I feel I will never be his equal." He described Yang's impact on his character to Edgar Snow: "He believed in his ethics very strongly and tried to imbue his students with the desire to become just, moral and virtuous men in society." The admiration was mutual. Yang commented that "it is truly difficult to find someone so intelligent and handsome …many unusual talents have come from peasant families."

Mao thus participated in many of the long hikes that Yang organized as well as the Sunday discussion sessions he held in his home. Yang presented attractive ideas of how liberalism and individualism could be used to create a democratic reimagining of Chinese society. He promoted the concept of strong individual personalities that arose from intense self-cultivation and encouraged his students to achieve self-actualization to help restore the nation's glory. These ideas would prove to be dangerous to Mao's fellow countrymen since they created the perilous logic that morality was relative, and thus could be set aside for the goals of a "strong individual" to pursue his own ends.

His thinking on the relationship between a political leader and the masses can be gleaned from his 1912 essay on Lord Shang Yang[xix], an ancient Chinese minister whose radical reforms had strengthened the state of Qin. Mao was ready to overlook the cruelties of his dictatorship (which led to a massive death count) on account that he had achieved considerable political power. He lamented the "ignorance" and "stupidity" of the Chinese masses for distrusting and fearing him.

Mao's concept of self-improvement and self-realization was not limited to his intellectual pursuits alone. Together with his classmates, he would pursue rigorous forms of physical and spiritual training as a form of preparation for their future endeavors as the nation's reformers. This included hiking through the fields and mountains, hiking along the city's walls, sun-bathing when the weather was hot, "wind bathing" when spring brought gusts of winds, swimming in the river during winter, and sleeping out in the open when it began to snow. Mao was shaping himself up to be the hero that China needed, ready to undo the humiliations inflicted by foreign powers and the injustices wrought by its long line of corrupt monarchs, court officials, feudal lords, oligarchs, and military leaders.

As Mao explored his dreams of political power and the strategies needed to maintain it, the nation's political situation became increasingly perilous. Yuan Shikai, the general who had been elected as the provisional president of the Republic of China, had died on June 6, 1916, because of uremia. His death occurred amid tumultuous times. Yuan's attempt to impose an explicitly dictatorial order in the nation had created conflict with Sun Yat-sen's revolutionaries and local military oligarchs. The Revolutionary Alliance (now known as the Guomindang, or Nationalist Alliance) openly opposed his rule and were outlawed in November 1913, forcing Sun Yat-Sen to flee to Japan. Yuan's decision to appease Japan's demands for Germany's territories in China after World War I began stirring anger and indignation across the nation. Yuan died as civil war consumed the country, and was replaced by General Li Yuanhong. As central power dissolved, provinces across the country – including Hunan, where

Mao was – plunged into chaos as local militarists fought for control amongst themselves.

In the fall of 1917, Mao decided the time for contemplation had given way to the time for action. He had been named the best student in his school in June 1917 and was beginning to demonstrate his organizational capacities. He became the leader of the Student Union and helped to restore the evening workers' school that provided classes for unemployed laborers in the city. In November that year, he helped to organize a student volunteer guard (with only bamboo sticks and wooden rifles) that would protect students – especially female ones – from improper behavior from soldiers. Mao even organized a defense against the army's demands to convert the school into a barracks. In April 1918, Mao helped to establish the Xinmin xuehui (Renovation of the People Study Society) to connect with other students who desired to improve the nation. The society aimed to make sense of the new modes of thinking that had appeared across the nation, and to achieve its lofty aim: "To improve the life of the individual and of the whole human race." Each member had to follow five simple rules:

"1. Do not be hypocritical;

2. Do not be lazy;

3. Do not be wasteful;

4. Do not gamble;

5. Do not consort with prostitutes".

Their sense of how to improve the "whole human race" was nevertheless far from defined. The group generally agreed on being anti-imperialist, but otherwise, their ideas flirted inconclusively with Kantianism, Confucianism, liberalism, utopianism, and democratic ideals in their quest to achieve national progress. When Mao graduated from the Normal School in June 1919, he was similarly devoid of a clear sense of what he wanted to do next. Instead of pursuing full-time work, he lived alongside the Xiang River with several friends and spent his time amongst nature.

Chapter 3 – Beijing

A letter from his favorite teacher Yang Changji, who was now working at Peking University, provided an alternative course of action. It detailed an attractive opportunity to study in democratic, revolutionary France – via the Chinese Society for Frugal Study in France, a work-study program that intended to help young Chinese citizens gain access to French education while working to pay for their expenses. The budding intellectuals would work alongside the workers and laborers, bridging the categorical gap between workers and intellectuals and eventually helping to rejuvenate China. Mao and his cadres were excited at the possibility of studying in France and made plans to travel to Beijing to confirm their participation.

Before leaving for Beijing, Mao visited his mother, Wen Qimei. She had been plagued by stomach ulcers for a long time and had recently developed inflammation of her lymph nodes. She had also decided to leave her husband to stay with her older brothers in her home village due to irreconcilable differences. Mao hoped she would travel to Changsha to benefit from medical testing, but she declined. He revealed his plans to visit Beijing without mentioning the possibility of studying in France.

In August 1919, Mao embarked on his first train ride to Beijing (from the neighboring city of Wuhan) with twenty-five of his comrades. There, Yang Changji agreed to accommodate Mao and three of his comrades in his home. Mao had met his teacher's daughter Yang

Kaihui before, as a young girl. She was now a young woman, and Mao was awestruck by her beauty. Kaihui had heard her father proclaim Mao's intelligence and accomplishments before and was similarly smitten. Neither party, however, were immediately transparent about their feelings.

After a few days, Mao relocated to a tiny apartment with three rooms with seven of his friends. They did not have enough money for heat, so they huddled close to each other at night for warmth. The apartment was near Peking University and the Forbidden City, providing Mao with easy access to some of the city's architectural and intellectual wonders. Peking University was the center of The New Culture Movement, which involved Chinese intellectuals parsing through various economic, political and social theories that would help to improve the nation. Traditional Confucian ideals were swept aside to make way for democracy, humanism, individualism, and liberalism. Mao was strongly attracted to *New Youth*, the journal of the moment, and the leaders of the movement: Cai Yuanpei, Rector Cai, Li Dazhao, Hu Shi and Chen Duxiu.

In October 1918, Professor Yang Changji secured him a job as an assistant librarian at Peking University. Mao would be working under Li Dazhao, director of the library and an economist, historian and philosopher. Li was one of the first intellectuals to consider how the new tenets of Marxism could be applied to China. Li was also one of China's first intellectuals to turn to the Bolshevik revolution in Russia as a chief source of inspiration. Li would personally familiarize Mao with Marxism and Bolshevik ideology once he began working in the university library. Mao would also be invited to participate in political activities. His intellectual horizons broadened, Mao decided to attend lecturers at Peking University and joined university societies focused on modern literature, journalism, and philosophy.

Despite his position under Li Dazhao, Mao would fall under the ideological spell of Chen Duxiu, the dean of the College of Letters.

He would reveal to Edgar Snow that Chen had influenced him "perhaps more than anyone else." Chen did not support Marxism or Bolshevism, believing instead in democracy, humanism and personal freedom. Mao's intellectual allegiance with Li meant he was distanced from Li's support for Bolshevism. He did, however, become personally interested in Peter Kropotkin's anarchism, partly because of the importance it placed on individualism. Mao's exposure to anarchist texts in the library – coupled with the fact that his arrival in Beijing was triggered by a French work-study program organized by anarchists – planted increasingly radical thoughts in his mind.

Unfortunately, his dreams of studying in France were hindered by his relative ineptitude at languages. To be selected for the program, he would have to pass a French language examination. He was also burdened by anxieties about his social status as an assistant librarian from the southern countryside. Mao was brought into the social and intellectual fold by Li Dazhao and Chen Duxiu, but many other established intellectuals at the university ignored him.

As some of his comrades embarked for France, Mao received news that his mother's health had worsened. Instead of departing immediately to her side, however, he made several detours. After leaving Beijing on March 12, he spent twenty days in Beijing with students who would soon be heading to France. He would arrive in Changsha on April 6 but waited until April 28 to write to his uncles to inform them that he was on his way home to Shaoshan. Wen Qimei would die on October 5, 1919, without seeing her son for the last time. Mao nevertheless arrived in time for her funeral and recited a poem he had written himself. When his father died less than four months later, Mao did not travel back home to attend his funeral[xx].

Chapter 4 – May Fourth and the New Culture Movement

Mao did not return immediately to Beijing after his mother's death. Instead, he began teaching history at Xiuye Primary School – a position he obtained with the help of an old friend. Mao lived in the school and received a low salary (four yuan per month), but this was sufficient to pay for his food and water.

Mao's return to Changsha coincided with the anti-imperialist May Fourth Movement in Beijing. On May 4th, 1919, vigorous student protests began after the Chinese government failed to defend its national interests in light of the terms drawn by the Treaty of Versailles. Germany had surrendered the port of Qingdao and the surrounding Jiaozhou Bay after the Siege of Tsingtao, and Japan was determined to gain control of the former German colony. England, Italy, and France had benefited from an allying with Japan during World War I and were relying on Japan to cooperate in an emerging war against Soviet Russia and thus supported Japan's bid for control over these areas[xxi].

The patriotic students were outraged and indignant that China would only be given some ancient astronomical instruments that the Germans had taken during the Boxer Rebellion. They were also appalled at the apparent presence of Chinese traitors who would allow such humiliating concessions for private profit. A fervent anti-Japanese patriotic movement began, targeted at high-ranking government officials who were suspected of betraying national interests. On May 4th, over three thousand students arrived at

Tiananmen Square with white flags (the color of mourning) to protest Japanese control over Qingdao[xxii]. When they were refused entry to the nearby Legation Quarter (with the aim of submitting a petition to the American minister), they headed over to the house of Cao Rulin, the minister of communications, to express their fury. Cao managed to escape, but Zhang Zongxiang, the Chinese minister to Tokyo, was physically assaulted by the students. Cao's house was eventually set on fire.

Their anti-Japanese sentiments resonated throughout the city during the following months. Rickshaw pullers, workers, merchants and members of the gentry demonstrated similarly patriotic feelings through strikes, demonstrations, and refusal of service to the Japanese in the country. Japanese goods were boycotted throughout China. Stores that traded and sold Japanese goods were vandalized. Mao would help organize such grassroots protest endeavors by a Hunan student association he co-organized. Cao Rulin, Zhang Zongxiang and Lu Zongyu (the director of the Chinese Mint) were forced to resign. It was only the news that Chinese delegates had declined to sign the Treaty of Versailles on June 28 that quelled the protests.

At this time, Mao decided that political propaganda would be a more effective means of informing, influencing, persuading and mobilizing the masses. Without the financial means to establish a newspaper, Mao and his comrades decided to form a Hunan-based student information journal titled *Xiangjiang pinglun* (Xiang River review). In its founding manifesto, Mao, the editor-in-chief, wrote "Unfettered by any of the old views or superstitions, we must seek the truth. In dealing with people, we advocate uniting the popular masses, and toward the oppressors, we believe in continuing the 'sincere admonishment movement.'" The oppressors he referred to include foreign imperialists such as Japan, bureaucrats, militarists, and capitalists. At this point, he believed in non-violent forms of protest, preferring the use of boycotts, strikes and peaceful protests.

Mao had been personally struck by the arrest of his intellectual idol Chen Duxiu by Beijing militarists after distributing a leaflet that contained harsh criticism of the government's domestic and foreign policies in relation to the ex-German colony. In his newly-founded journal, he attributed the arrest to critical deficits in the nation's mental faculties:

"The real danger lies in the total emptiness and rottenness of the mental universe of the entire Chinese people. Of China's 400 million people, about 390 million are superstitious. They superstitiously believe in spirits and ghosts, in fortune-telling, in fate, in despotism. There is absolutely no recognition of the individual, of the self, of truth. This is because scientific thought has not developed. In name, China is a republic, but in reality, it is an autocracy that is getting worse and worse as one regime replaces another …[The} masses of the people haven't the faintest glimmer of democracy in their mentality and have no idea what democracy actually is[xxiii]."

His attempt at publishing had been tremendously successful. By the time his fourth issue was sold on August 4, it had an initial print run of five thousand copies. Mao would write articles, edit it himself, proofread and compose the printer's dummy himself, and occasionally even sold copies on the street. Its pages would host the article that earned him national recognition: "The Great Union of the Popular Masses." In this ambitious essay, which spanned three separate issues, Mao addressed the ultimate question that had swirled in his mind all these years: what revolutionaries of this generation should do when "the decadence of the state, the sufferings of humanity, and the darkness of society have all reached an extreme." He argued that the masses needed to unite against the aristocrats and capitalists to combat the violence of oppression and proposed that trade unions be formed to protect the interests of the poor, vulnerable and weak. Given their greater numbers, the aristocrats and capitalists would be unable to defend themselves against a mass uprising – as had occurred during the 1917 Russian Revolution[xxiv]. He also implored Chinese soldiers to switch allegiances to the popular masses and help usher in a more just society. The article was well received in the cities, with even Beijing intellectuals who had ignored him when he was a librarian's assistant lavishing praise.

Emboldened, Mao organized political activity against Zhang Jingyao, the corrupt, violent, and exploitative governor of Hunan. He was also invited by the Sino-American hospital Xiangya to serve as the editor in chief of its weekly journal *New Hunan.* As with his *Xiang River Review,* the publication of the *New Hunan* was soon halted by the authorities.

As Mao's fame and popularity grew, so did his appeal to the opposite sex. At twenty-five, he embarked on his first romantic affair. While Yang Kaihui was in Beijing, Mao pursued a romance with her father's favorite female student, Tao Yi. The two bonded over their shared passions for liberalism, democracy, and free love. Having been forced into an unwanted arranged marriage himself, Mao was a firm believer in individual choice in matters of romance and marriage[xxv]. The two soon went separate ways, however. By 1920, Mao had begun to firmly embrace the tenets of communism. Tao Yi found herself incapable of supporting Bolshevism. She left for Shanghai soon after they broke up and founded a women's school there.

As their romance unfolded and dissolved, Mao was determined to rally opposition against Zhang. In November 1920, he held a meeting to revive the Renovation of the People Study Society. By organizing it into two clearly defined departments (a legislative and executive department) and forming an Executive Committee, the loose coalition of individuals began to resemble a centralized political party. After nearly a year of inactivity, the organization decided to hold a public burning of a significant quantity of contraband Japanese goods that they uncovered while inspecting a warehouse in Changsha. This demonstration was thwarted by Zhang's military troops, who were led by his younger brother Zhang Jingtang. His soldiers overpowered the student protesters, beat them, and forced them to vacate the town square.

Mao and his comrades decided to retaliate by organizing a national campaign to oust Zhang. Strikes began on December 6, with seventy-three out of seventy-five of the schools shutting down. Teachers and students insisted on staying away from the school until Zhang was unseated from political power in Hunan. Mao also organized a delegation to Beijing to pressure the president's administration, his cabinet and various ministers to exert their influence to punish and remove Zhang because of the corruption, theft, rape, violence, and murders he had committed. The government had no real intentions of dealing with Zhang and merely promised that a "secret investigation" was underway. Zhang would remain in power until 1920, only to have his position of governor occupied by another warlord.

He also suffered another blow while in Beijing. Upon arrival, he learnt that his beloved professor Yang Changji had been suffering from terminal stomach cancer. He met Yang Kaihui again at her father's bedside and helped to establish a fund to support his family after he died while leaving them little financial support.

Inspiration nevertheless came with news of the Bolshevik Revolution in Russia. Mao began to explore Marxist texts after learning the Bolshevik Party had been successful in unifying peasants and workers against the aristocrats and plutocrats that he resented. During this time, Mao perused abbreviated translations of the *The Communist Manifesto*, *The Critique of the Gotha Programme,* Vladimir Lenin's "Political Parties in Russia and the Tasks of the Proletariat", Leon Trotsky's "Manifesto of the Communist International to the Proletariat of the World", Karl Kautsky's *Class Struggle,* and Thomas Kirkup's *A History of Socialism*. The October Revolution in Russia prompted widespread interest in Marxist theories in China, but many leading intellectuals only focused on Bolshevism instead of the broader spectrum of Marxist thought. Mao was not singularly interested in Marxism, however. He also studied the works of liberal intellectuals like Henri Bergson, Bertrand Russell, John Dewey while dabbling with linguistics and Buddhism.

On April 11, 1920, Mao embarked on a journey from Beijing to Tianjin, Jinan (capital of the Shandong province), Qufu (the birthplace of Confucius), and to the summit of the holy mountain of Taishan. He visited Zoucheng (the birthplace of Mencius), before heading to Nanjing, and then to Shanghai. There, he spent half his time earning money by working as a laundryman and the other half discussing politics and walking through the city. He would have become well-acquainted with the city's cosmopolitan character, given the presence of many Europeans, Americans, Japanese, French citizens, and Russians in the International Settlement. He continued to advocate for positive political change in Hunan for advancing the idea of an "independent Hunan," freed from the rule of the northern government. When he visited his intellectual idol Chen Duxiu to discuss his ideas of secession, however, he found that Chen was being courted by Comintern agents to establish an alliance with Soviet Russia and disseminate communist ideas within China.

Left uncertain about this development, Mao returned to Hunan and decided to form a cooperative bookstore with his friends. The Cultural Book Society was meant to enrich the people of Hunan with affordable books, journals, and newspapers that advanced social and political literature. This included works by Darwin, Plato, Marxist texts, and Mao's personal favorites. The store was a success. More branches opened in seven districts across Hunan by April 1921. Within the same quarters as the bookstore, Mao founded the Russia Studies Society. Its goal was to organize the collective study of Soviet Russia, publish research and reviews of the nation and its ideology, and fund a Russian language class for those who intended to travel to Moscow for further study. Mao would learn Russian in the hopes of studying in Russia.

He also continued to advocate for an independent Hunan, but the petitions, agitation, numerous articles, meetings, and demonstrations failed to catalyze any revolution. Mao was disheartened by the passivity and apathy of the general population to the cause for reform and began to see the appeal of Bolshevism. By July 1920, Chen Duxiu was heading a communist cell in Shanghai. By August, the Shanghai Socialist Youth League had been formed. After other such organizations materialized in other cities, the Socialist Youth of China was officially announced. The nation's first communists were not workers or peasants. They were mainly students, journalists and young teachers who all aimed to emulate the Russian Revolution in their homeland as soon as the opportunity arose. Chen, the oldest member of the group, began propagating communist ideals and Marxist theory to influence fellow intellectuals as well as the workers.

Mao began to see the utility of Bolshevism at this time. His experiences with political movements on a grassroots level had left him disillusioned with the idea of everyday Chinese citizens rising above centuries of the feudal rule to engender self-government. The Bolsheviks had succeeded in Russia with a totalitarian dictatorship by the ruling communist party, which curtailed civic freedoms instead of encouraging it. At the time, 390 million (out of 400 million) of Chinese citizens were illiterate. The monarchical rule had been abolished in 1912, but they had no understanding of what living in a republic meant. Bolshevik-style communism would appeal to the masses by virtue of its ideals of universal equality, but it would simultaneously allow the leaders of the communist party with uncontested power. Meanwhile, it would also capture the imagination of the young revolutionaries with its grand narrative of class struggle and ultimate aim of having the workers overthrow their oppressive capitalist overlords. In China, a proletariat revolution would rise against several forces: (1) the familiar feudal-militarist forces; (2) the new and emerging capitalist bourgeoisie; (3) the imperialist foreign powers who wielded foreign capital and influence in China.

When Mao was appointed as the director of a primary school that was part of the Provincial First Normal School, he gained the benefits of a considerable salary for the first time in his life. He also had access to a pool of impressionable young people he could recruit into the growing ranks of the Hunan chapter of the Socialist Youth League. He also needed to persuade the other members of the Renovation of the People Study Society to accept the tenets of Bolshevism, and thereby orient its political compass towards communism.

As Mao enjoyed steady success in convincing additional people to convert to communism, he also made a significant step in his romantic life. After Yang Changji's death, Yang Kaihui returned to Changsha with her mother and brother in January 1920 to bury his coffin where he was born (in Bancang, a small town north of Changsha). Kaihui then continued her studies in Changsha. Mao and Kaihui began a slow courtship, which involved long walks along the river. Instead of directly talking about their feelings for each other, they discussed politics, the Bolshevik revolution, and Marxist thought. Kaihui eventually joined the Socialist Youth League due to Mao's influence. In the winter of 1920, they were married. They omitted the rituals of a traditional Chinese marriage ceremony (the dowry, the red palanquin), which they deemed to be "petty bourgeois philistinism.[xxvi]"

In January 1921, the Renovation of the People Study Society held an important meeting that would decide their political and ideological orientation from then on. They debated on the merits of social policy, moderate communism, anarchism, radicalism, and social democracy. They eventually agreed the Russian form of socialism would be best-suited to China since dictatorship could be used to force change onto a relatively apathetic population.

Instead of rejoicing at this momentous occasion, Mao fell into despair (possibly as a result of all the stress he had endured as he arrived at this moment). In a letter he penned to a friend at this point, he excoriated himself (a highly atypical occurrence) for all the "defects" that prevented him for becoming the great leader he had always aspired to become[xxvii]. He listed eight specific character flaws: (1) he was overly emotional; (2) he often resorted to subjective judgments; (3) he was fairly narcissistic; (4) he was often too arrogant; (5) he seldom analyzed his own mistakes, typically blaming others when things went wrong; (6) he excelled at lofty rhetoric, but was deficient when it came to systematic analysis; (7) he had an over-inflated sense of his accomplishments; (8) his will was not as iron-willed as he had assiduously shaped it to be. This moment of intense self-doubt did not last long.

Chapter 5 – The Communist Party of China's Growing Pains

On 29 June 1921, Mao left Changsha for Shanghai to attend the founding congress of the Chinese Communist Party (CCP[xxviii]). At this time, Sun Yat-Sen had been appointed as the president of the Republic of China – a signal that a new era was at hand. The path ahead was nevertheless far from certain. There were only fifty-three people in the CCP at this point. At the meeting, Mao Zedong was appointed as the party secretary. The core principles of the CCP were laid out during this meeting[xxix]:

I. The proletariat would stage a revolution to unseat the capitalist class, forming a new nation devoid of class distinctions.

II. A dictatorship of the proletariat was to be formed to achieve the final stage of the class struggle.

III. All private ownership of capital and the productive means of society (machines, factories, land, buildings, etc.) were to be replaced by social ownership.

IV. As a communist nation, China would unite with the Third International (also known as The Communist International), the international communist organization that advocated for world communism.

The delegates were nevertheless in conflict with the Comintern representatives who attended the meeting. They did not accept the idea that Chinese communists should be temporarily allied with the more bourgeois nationalists (i.e. Sun Yat-Sen) in organizing a national revolution. The Comintern agents in China thus had to convince their Chinese counterparts to engage the KMT (Kuomintang[xxx]) instead of attempting to stage a proletariat revolution on their own.

Like the majority of his comrades, Mao was opposed to the idea of the CCP cooperating with the KMT to achieve its goals. After returning to Changsha, Mao founded the Hunan branch of the All-China Workers' Secretariat with the aim of catalyzing a worker's movement under the influence of the CCP. With the help of local anarchists, he organized a two-thousand-worker strike in April 1921, at a cotton mill in Changsha. He convinced the two key leaders of Hunan's Labor Association of the importance of instilling a class consciousness, and they eventually joined the Socialist Youth League[xxxi]. When both were executed by the thugs working for the new Hunan governor Zhao Hengti, Mao was able to assume leadership of the workers' movement in the province.

There may have only been three large industrial enterprises in the entire Hunan province, but Mao was still keen on realizing Marx's vision of a worker-led revolution. Mao considered the coolies, rickshaw pullers, and seasonal laborers to all fall under the category of "workers." As 1923 unfolded, Mao successfully organized twenty-two trade unions with the help of his comrades. They were unions for miners, railway workers, typographers, rickshaw pullers, barbers, municipal service workers, etc[xxxii]. A fervent labor movement had begun, climaxing in many strikes that aimed to increase their wages, reduce their working hours from twelve hours per day to eight hours per day, and improve their working conditions. Mao was personally involved in the organization of many of these strikes and would give rousing speeches to inspire and mobilize the miners, railroad and factory workers across the nation. He also recruited his wife, his two younger brothers, his second cousin and his second cousin's wife to join the CCP and help him stir the worker's movement onward. He appointed his middle brother Zemin to become the bursar at the primary school he directed. His younger brother Zetan was appointed as the secretary of the municipal committee of the Chinese Socialist Youth League.

The successes of many of the strikes Mao organized helped him gain major support among the workers. When the Hunan Federation of Trade Unions (HFTU) was founded on November 5, 1922, Mao was elected as its general secretary[xxxiii]. With his newfound influence, Mao was able to pressure Governor Zhao Hengti to recognize the workers' constitutional rights to organize themselves and to strike. Mao and his comrades were nevertheless unsuccessful in converting the workers to communism. The vast majority of workers were apolitical, and not immediately radicalized despite participating in strikes to improve their working conditions. Mao had to rely on other means of opposing the governor.

On October 10, 1921, Mao was elected as the secretary as the Hunan committee of the CCP. When the Special Xiang District Committee formed under the dictate of the CCP's Central Bureau in May 1922, Mao was elected secretary. He was also the head of the Socialist Youth League of Changsha's Executive Committee. He had already been serving as the general manager of the Self-Study University he founded in Changsha (after resigning from his headmaster position at the primary school he was working at) by August that year. He was beginning to monopolize the power of this underground Bolshevik movement and would exert an unparalleled influence over the newly recruited communists and socialists within the region.

In early 1922, five delegates from the First CCP Congress visited Moscow and Petrograd to attend the first Congress of the Peoples of the Far East, upon invitation from the Bolshevik leaders. There, they were persuaded to cooperate with the nationalist revolutionaries in order to emancipate the millions of struggling Chinese citizens. This time, the Russians were successful in convincing the CCP to unite with the nationalist revolutionaries in opposing the imperialists and militarists. There was some opposition, but the CCP ultimately resolved to form a temporary alliance with the KMT. They were, after all, reliant on financial support from Moscow to fund all their activities. With Sun Yat-sen's endorsement, the proletariat, the peasants, and the national bourgeoisie would thus be united in opposing foreign imperialism and the corrupt Peking government. The communists would not join the KMT and would retain their independence.

As Mao organized strikers and demonstrations in Hunan, Sun Yat-Sen and leaders of the CCP arranged meetings to discuss the structure, nature, and content of their alliance. Sun's famous Three Principles of the People (also known as the Three Great Principles) were reformulated as nationalism (self-definition for the Chinese people), socialism (people's livelihood) and democracy (the rights of the people)[xxxiv]. Sun also agreed to have the KMT mirror the CCP's alignment with Russia.

Mao became a father on October 21, 1922. He named his first son Anying, which means "The Hero Who Reaches the Shore of Socialism." He had little opportunity to care for his newborn son. On February 7, the militarist Wu Peifu initiated a bloody retaliation against the railroad workers on strike. With thirty-two workers killed, two hundred wounded and many workers' clubs and trade unions under threat, Mao was compelled to take swift and decisive action. The next day, he organized a general strike on the Changsha-Wuchang railroad as twenty thousand workers and students attended a memorial meeting for those who had been killed. Other urban trade unions organized meetings, while a major demonstration occurred at the Anyuan mines. The following month, Mao sponsored a major anti-Japanese demonstration in his capacity as the head of the Special Xiang District Committee. Over sixty thousand people marched through the streets of Changsha, demanding that Japan return the Chinese territories it had control over. In April, Hunan Governor Zhao

Hengti retaliated against Mao and the union leaders. With an arrest warrant on his head, Mao was forced to escape.

His superiors in the CCP were pleased with the progress he had made and were happy to have him replicate what he had achieved in other provinces. His wife Kaihui was pregnant with his second child as he departed for Shanghai, without any inkling of when she would see him again. From Shanghai, Mao headed to Canton as the CCP's Central Executive Committee relocated. The experience of witnessing the deaths of the Hankou railway workers and Zhao Hengti's violent retaliation against the workers' movement in Hunan had convinced Mao that allying with Sun's Canton government was necessary for victory. Sun Yat-Sen's government in Canton had provided support to the Chinese workers and Hong Kong seamen who went on a similar strike, allowing them to achieve far more success than the communist-backed Hunan workers had achieved.

During the Third Congress of the Communist Party from June 12-20, 1923, Mao ultimately agreed with the majority on having the CCP help the KMT expand its support base outside of Canton. With the working class being relatively small, the CCP would not be able to become a mass organization in the immediate future. Mao was also elected as a member of the Central Executive Committee (CEC) for the first time. He was made the head of the Organizational Department and secretary of the CEC. He had risen through the ranks and was now the second in command in the party – second only to his idol Chen Duxiu. His reputation for being a capable writer, thinker, and grassroots leader had even reached Moscow. At this time, he began to envision the power that could be gained by mobilizing the landless peasants against the powerful landowners.

As the Comintern agents, the CCP and the KMT further clarified the political front they were uniting on; Mao moved to Shanghai at Chen Duxiu's request. He still supported the alliance with the KMT but was wary of the possibility of the CCP being wholly subsumed by the larger organization. At the time, he defined the political problem as "the problem of the national revolution. To use the might of the people to overthrow the warlords and to overthrow foreign imperialism, which colludes with the warlords in their evil acts – such is the historic mission of the Chinese people ... We must all have faith that the one and only way to save oneself and the nation is the national revolution[xxxv]."

In September, Mao headed to Changsha to establish a KMT branch. His communist comrades resisted the idea, and his objective was made even more difficult when Governor Zhao Hengti declared martial law in the Hunan province. He also ordered for Mao and the other leaders of the labor movement to be arrested. Mao's second son Anqing was born at this trying time. His named means "The Youth Who Reaches the Shore of Socialism." In January 1924, Mao left his family for Shanghai once again to attend Sun Yat-Sen's Unification Congress of the KMT as a delegate from Hunan. The congress' main outcome was the formation of a united front, with the communists gained full admission to the KMT. There were nevertheless many contradictions and points of conflict between the communists and Sun Yat-Sen's followers. Meanwhile, Mao's health had begun to deteriorate under the strain of his workload. His place of residence in the dirty, smoke-filled small town of Zhabei had also contributed to his declining health. He resigned from his position as secretary of the Organizational Department. In December that year, he requested medical leave from the CCP Central Executive Committee. Mao and his family left Shanghai for Changsha. He would spend seven months there and did not return to Shanghai to attend the Fourth Congress of the CCP, which took place in January 1925. His decision to stay out of the fray indicated his intolerance for the politicking between the communists and the "bourgeois nationalists," as well as the constant interference from Moscow. Mao was not re-elected to the new Central Executive Committee.

During his time away from the city, Mao began to spread Marxist ideas and Bolshevism among the peasants of his clan. With the help of his family members, he established over twenty peasant unions by the spring of 1925. As an intellectual, Mao saw himself as being a class above the illiterate peasants who had toiled on the land for centuries. He nevertheless relished the opportunity to rally them together and became more assured of his initial vision of having the vast peasantry lead the revolution he had been waiting for.

On March 12 that year, Sun Yat-Sen died of liver cancer in Beijing, where he was to attend a peace conference that would discuss how best to unify the country. After a brief power struggle within the KMT, the party's "leftists" prevailed. Wang Jingwei, who had been the head of the Propaganda Department of the CEC, replaced Sun as the leader of the KMT and the head of the government in Canton.

On 30th May that same year, a surge of intense nationalism erupted in Shanghai. British troops had fired at a crowd of protesters, who were agitating over the murder of Gu Zhenghong, a communist worker, by a Japanese man. Gu's murder had led to major protests and another wave of anti-Japanese sentiment, which intensified when Chinese militarists in Qingdao heeded the wishes of Japanese entrepreneurs and fired at the protesting workers, killing two of them and wounding sixteen others. The events in Qingdao catalyzed two thousand students to gather on Nanking Road, within the International Settlement, and to protest the presence of all imperial powers in the nation. The police officers ended up killing ten of them and wounding many others, causing even more agitation and fury. The death count only increased when American, Italian and British warships arrived via Huangpu River after two hundred thousand Shanghai workers went on strike. Forty-one Chinese citizens were killed and 120 were wounded[xxxvi].

These events led to the May Thirtieth Movement. Nation-wide strikes, protest meetings, boycotts, demonstrations, and a mass migration of workers from the colonial centers of Shanghai, Shamian, and Hong

Kong transpired. The KMT government supported these strikes by declaring a blockade of Hong Kong and Shamian and forming the Hong Kong-Shamian Strike Committee. As the revolutionary forces magnetized the entire nation, the CCP-KMT alliance began to exude a more powerful appeal.

In his home village of Shaoshan, Mao rallied the peasant unions around the cause of patriotism and anti-imperialism. Peasants were now introduced to the idea of boycotting foreign goods. When Mao organized the peasants against a local wealthy farmer named Chen, however, he prompted Governor Zhao Hengti to announce a new order for his arrest. Mao had opposed Chen's refusal to sell grain from his reserves to the peasants, who were afraid of starving due to a drought (he would be able to sell them at a greater price in the city). Mao had rallied over a hundred peasants to march to Chen's warehouse with bamboo poles and hoes, demanding to buy the grain at a fair price. Chen was forced to agree, but quickly informed Zhao of Mao's actions.

Mao fled for Changsha and then headed south to Canton. Mao had suffered a nervous attack during his trip and had to spend two weeks in Dongshan Hospital as he recovered. The news of a scandalous series of romantic betrayals within the CCP's upper echelon only worsened his condition. Kaihui's arrival in Canton with her mother and their children soon afterward helped him recuperate.

Chapter 6 – The Northern Expedition

In the earlier half of 1926, the efforts of the CCP and Comintern to exert a greater communist influence over the GMD (Chinese Nationalist Party) led to an anti-leftist military coup led by Chiang Kai-shek[xxxvii]. In March that year, Chiang would no longer pretend to be aligned with the CCP or the Soviet Union. Chiang declared martial law, had several communists arrested, and mobilized his trips to patrol the homes of many Soviet military advisers. He publicly announced his position as thus: "I believe in communism and am almost a communist myself, but the Chinese communists have sold out to the Russians and become 'their dogs.' Therefore, I oppose them[xxxviii]." Chiang's coup was peaceful, but it also firmly established a military dictatorship and compromised the positions of the communists and KMT "leftists." Chiang also demanded the political and organizational autonomy of the communists within the KMT be restricted. He began to monopolize power within the party by having himself appointed as the chairman of the Standing Committee of the Guomindang CEC, the head of the National Government's Military Council, the head of the KMT CEC's Department of Military Cadres, and the commander in chief of the National Revolutionary Army. Given that Stalin wished that the CCP remain within the KMT and buy their time, the CCP was forced to accept their diminished positions.

As a result, Mao was forced to resign from his post in the KMT CEC. He focused his energies on organizing the Chinese peasantry with his newfound position as the director of the Sixth Session of the Peasant Movement Training Institute. By then, he had gained a reputation as the foremost expert on the question of how to involve the peasantry in the revolution amongst the KMT leaders and the CCP. Through his writings, Mao advocated that the peasants, sharecroppers, farm laborers and vagrants revolt against the entire landlord class, who he deemed to be equivalent to the despised imperialists, militarists, and bureaucrats.

When March ended, Chiang had made the necessary preparations for his Northern Expedition: a military campaign to pacify the militarist in the north and to ultimately unify China[xxxix]. Over 100,000 officers from the National Revolutionary Army headed north to engage the three groups of militarists who stood in opposition to Chiang Kai-shek: Wu Peifu, Marshal Sun Chuanfang, and Marshal Zhang Zuolin. While Wu and Sun's armies each surpassed 200,000 officers, Zhang had approximately 350,000 men. Luck was nevertheless on Chiang's side. An army division within Wu's coalition, led by commander Tang Shengzhi, had defected to Canton. Chiang mobilized his officers to rally around Tang, and the latter's officers were regrouped as the NRA's Eighth Corps.

In 1926, the NRA had achieved a major victory by assuming control of Wuhan. The National government was relocated from Canton to Wuhan. On the first day of 1927, Wuhan was declared the capital of Kuomintang China. As the NRA took over and occupied many provinces, the peasants became emboldened to act on their burgeoning class consciousness. By December 1926, the number of peasants who had joined the numerous peasant organizations available had increased from 400,000 to 1.3 million[xl]. They attacked and destroyed the homes of the rich landowners across the countryside, seeking revenge for the years of humiliation and exploitation that had endured at the hands of their wealthier counterparts. Anyone who owned land, however insignificant in size, was deemed to be a member of the gentry and greatly suspect. In their wake, all signs of wealth – pools filled with expensive fish, ornate furniture, artworks, and jewelry – were either destroyed or stolen. When asked to prepare a report for this unprecedented uprising, Mao condoned the excessive violence and terror as a necessary part of the revolution. Tensions within the KMT – between the communists and Chiang's "rightists" - intensified. The NRA overthrew the warlord Sun Chuanfang on March 21 and claimed Nanjing two days later.

At this time, Mao was also basking in success. His idea for a redistribution of land in the countryside – a radical suggestion – had been approved by the CCP and the KMT. In April Mao was included in the CEC's Land Committee to implement measures that would facilitate the transfer of land to the peasants. He also welcomed the birth of his third son with Kaihui. Mao named him Anlong, which meant "Dragon Who Reaches the Shore of Socialism."

The NRA eventually encountered a setback when they attacked the residence of important foreigners in Nanjing. In retaliation, the British and American ships shelled at the army. The NRA was also participating in an increasing number of conflicts with trade union organizations, and worker and peasant coalitions who had armed themselves. The peasants and workers had indiscriminately revolted against all landlords, even the medium-sized and petty ones that formed the foundation of the KMT. The NRA sought their revenge for arrested, assaulted and murdered family members against the masses, killing thousands in horrible ways. The NRA also turned on the communists. On April 28, Mao received the crushing news that Professor Li Dazhao and nineteen leaders from the Northern Bureau of the CCP had been tortured and then executed. Before long, the CCP was defeated by Chiang's forces.

As the CCP was in dire straits, it was Mao who concluded the communists would only secure power in China if it could brandish its own military force. His famed quote endures: "We must know that political power is obtained from the barrel of the gun." He recommended a strategic retreat to buy enough time to train an army of paupers, peasants, workers, and the landless. After Chen Duxiu sunk into depression when the KMT executed his eldest son, Qu Qiubai replaced him as the leader of the CCP. He agreed with Mao's suggestion that the CCP retreat into the mountains. On July 15, there would be little choice: all communists were expelled from the KMT. The communists attempted to battle the KMT soldiers with the Workers' and Peasants' Red Army of China (the "Red Army"[xli]), but they were forced to accept defeat by September 15. They headed east, to the Jinggang Mountains in Jiangxi.

Chapter 7 – Communists at Large

Mao bid farewell to Kaihui as he departed, as she would not be following the Red Army to Jiangxi. She would head with their children and their nanny to her mother's home in Bancang instead. She would never see him again and expressed her longing for his company in a poem: "Not even a letter of even a note from you. No one to ask how you are./ If I had wings, I'd fly to see you./ To pine forever for one's love is torture. When shall we two meet again?[xlii]" There, she was eventually pressured by the KMT commander to renounce her husband publicly. When she refused, she was sentenced to death on November 14, 1930.

When Mao heard the news a month later, he sent his mother-in-law thirty silver yuan for a gravestone. He somberly wrote, "The death of Kaihui cannot be repaid even should I die a hundred deaths." Mao's actions did not match his words. He had married a local interpreter, He Zizhen, only four months after leaving his wife and three sons. Like Kaihui, who had heard of Mao's remarriage two years before her execution, Zizhen (who was only eighteen when she first met Mao) would eventually learn her husband was incapable of fidelity.

Mao's refuge in Jinggang (which directly translated to "wells and ridges") housed over a thousand men and officers at the foot of the tallest mountain in the vicinity. There, he organized them into the Assembly of Workers, Peasants, and Soldier's Deputies (a legislative body) and the People's Assembly (an executive organ). By forming an alliance with the outlaws in the region, he was able to solidify his power in the region. As the KMT decimated the communists in the urban areas, many of them fled to the countryside.

His power within the CCP was nevertheless slipping. The Central Committee expelled him from their ranks for his "military opportunism," i.e. a lack of faith in the strength of the masses to accomplish the revolution. He was also dismissed from his other responsibilities in the party and demoted to the post of commander of the First Division. This left him without the power to contribute to discussions on political and military questions. His appointment as the secretary of the Hunan-Jiangxi Special Border Area Committee allowed him to monopolize power in the Jinggang region.

In May 1928, the number of communist fighters in Jinggang had grown to eighteen thousand. Mao took to the task of organizing them into disciplined soldiers. To obtain the resources needed to supply them with clothing, food, medicine, and weapons, he decided to implement a radical land redistribution scheme. He confiscated all the land that belonged to landlords and peasants and Jinggang and then redistributed it to the rural villagers who supported the communist regime. Those who received the land were compelled to work on it. The Red Army soldiers gained more military experience as they took down the local landlords and gentry that opposed the policy.

By the end of the year, Mao and the Red Army were compelled to leave their strategic base in the mountains. All the resources in the vicinity had been used up. Many of the local villagers and industries had been decimated as people fled to escape Mao's militarized version of communism. Only six thousand soldiers remained.

Mao relocated his base to the southern province of Jiangxi, along the Jiangxi-Fujian border. They would be far from the urban centers controlled by the KMY, with a local population that was sympathetic towards the communists. KMT troops were hunting them down, prompting them to take an irregular course. The Red Army claimed to protect the interests of the workers and peasants but made exploitative demands from the merchants and rich peasants they encountered.

In May 1929, He Zizhen gave birth to Mao's first daughter. He named her Jinhua ("Gold Flower"), and then insisted she hand her over to a peasant family for fifteen yuan. He promised Zizhen they would be able to find her after the revolution, but they would never see her again.

Mao's Red Army was dwindling, but he was able to make the most of his soldiers by perfecting his guerilla tactics. Militarized communists would adopt these successful military tactics in many other Asian, African and South American countries. By using them deftly, Mao was able to resist the KMT soldiers and antagonize opposing locals. He was able to implement his land redistribution policy in Jiangxi, as he had done in Jinggang. The Red Army destroyed tax offices and killed tax collectors alongside the gentry, officials, KMT members, priests, missionaries and the militarists.

On October 4, 1930, Mao took control over the Ji'an, a commercial city in Jiangxi, and announced the formation of the Jiangxi Provincial Soviet Government[xliii]. The Red Army obtained significant funds from the rich townspeople and were able to settle comfortably in the area. Mao's military successes had earned him the approval of Stalin, who saw the Red Army has being crucial for a communist victory in China.

The communists in Jiangxi soon began engaging in infighting, as the native people of Jiangxi viewed the Red Army as outsiders and opposed Mao's radical land reforms. By the end of October, Mao's Red Army would execute over a thousand Jiangxi communists. Before long, Mao also had to contend with increased aggression from the KMT army. His guerilla tactics ("the enemy advances, we retreat; the enemy camps, we harass; the enemy tires, we attack; the enemy retreats, we pursue[xliv]") was nevertheless able to defeat the KMT's first two attempts to encircle and annihilate the Red Army. Chiang

Kai-shek himself would eventually be compelled to travel to Jiangxi and lead the charge against the communists.

When the Japanese began pursuing an increasingly comprehensive expansionist policy in the region, however, Chiang was forced to retreat from Jiangxi. The Japanese occupied Mukden, Manchuria's largest city, on September 18, 1931[xlv]. With their formidable disciple and weapons, they assumed control of the entirety of Manchuria and its population of thirty million people by late fall. In the meantime, Mao solidified his power over the region and worked to redirect the wave of anti-Japanese fervor against Chiang, who had not defended Manchuria against the Japanese. He was now facing not only Chiang's forces, but also opponents within the party, class enemies that opposed communism, and comrades who disagreed with or opposed him. Mao announced that the Soviet government of China had officially declared war against the Japanese (even though the communist armies were nowhere near Manchuria and Shanghai). This propaganda was nevertheless effective in creating an image of genuine nationalism for the communists.

With its increasing popularity and mass support, the Red Army was eventually able to exert control over a population of 3 million people. Mao could pursue his land reform program, besides organizing education programs and introducing measures to recruit more women to join the CCP.

Chapter 8 – The Long March

Chiang deemed the communists to be a greater threat than the encroaching Japanese. In the years between 1930 and 1934, he would rally no less than five different military encirclement campaigns with the aim of eradicating the pesky communists once and for all. In his fifth encirclement campaign, he managed to deliver a devastating blow to the communist forces by personally mobilizing 700,000 of his men and forming a series of fortifications (in the form of cement blockhouses) around communist positions.

Mao's leadership had been revoked by the CCP's Central Committee in early 1934, resulting in the Red Army abandoning his preferred guerrilla warfare strategy. This was a near-fatal mistake: many communist soldiers were lost after they attempted to face the larger and better-equipped KMT army with positional warfare strategies. The communists were forced to flee for their lives in October. At the beginning of the march, 86,000 male and female communists in Jiangxi (soldiers and administrative personnel) broke through the weakest points of the KMT encirclement and headed towards the west. Zizhen accompanied Mao, but they had to leave their newborn son Anhong with Zizhen's sister He Yi. They would never see him again.

In the beginning, they were forced to contend with multiple attacks from Chiang's ground troops, as well as constant bombardment from his air force. By the time they arrived in Zunyi, in the southwestern province of Guizhou, their morale had plunged, and the Red Army had lost more than half of its ranks. Mao had not been in charge during the beginning of the retreat, but he gained enough support to establish his uncontested dominance of the party in January 1935.

He rallied the remaining troops to head toward the northwest, to gain the security of being closer to the security border. This would also mean the communists would be near the Japanese-occupied territory in northeastern China. In June, Mao's forces merged with the communist troops that had been operating in the Sichuan-Shaanxi border area under the leadership of Zhang Guotao[xlvi]. This led to a power struggle between Mao and Zhang for control of the central army in northern Sichuan. The main army eventually split into two factions, with Zhang's section heading towards the southwest. Mao led most of the troops towards northern Shaanxi, where there was a communist base to welcome them.

When he arrived there in October 1935, only 8,000 people had survived the march[xlvii]. Many had died from fighting the KMT, starvation and from diseases. Some had abandoned the march to rally the peasants along the way. Mao would proclaim his troops had covered 12,500 km, but British historians have argued they travelled only 6,000 km[xlviii]. In any case, Mao and his troops had to navigate some of the most challenging trails in the world, taking them across 18 mountain ranges and 24 rivers. They also had to contend with Chiang's forces nearly every step of the way, although they did not have to face the force of the entire KMT army (which was preoccupied with the Japanese Occupation before the March began).

The CCP was happy to capitalize on the compelling heroism that was attributed to the Long March. News of the communists' epic struggle to resist the KMT inspired many young Chinese men and women to travel to Shaanxi to enlist in Mao's Red Army. When the Japanese withdrew from China after their defeat in World War II (1939-45) to the United States, the CCP confronted the KMT once again. In 1949, the KMT was decisively defeated. Mao heralded the founding of the People's Republic of China on October 1, 1949[xlix].

Chapter 9 – The People's Republic of China

The CCP was happy to capitalize on the compelling heroism that was attributed to the Long March. News of the communists' epic struggle to resist the KMT inspired many young Chinese men and women to travel to Shaanxi to enlist in Mao's Red Army. When the Japanese withdrew from China after their defeat in World War II (1939-45) to the United States, the CCP confronted the KMT once again. In 1949, the KMT was decisively defeated. Mao heralded the founding of the People's Republic of China on October 1, 1949.

His early years at the helm of the country were a great success. During this time, the CCP steered the country towards economic growth and greater political strength[l]. After years of military rule under the warlords, the KMT army, and the Red Army, the people of China could finally live under civilian rule. Mao's effective leadership of the CCP during the early years was critical in establishing widespread confidence in its ability to govern the nation.

In October 1950, the PLA troops (the Chinese People's Volunteers) participated in the Korean War[li] against the forces of the UN. The "Resist America, aid Korea" campaign was effective in stirring patriotism across the nation, besides restoring confidence in the nation's military capacities after decades of military humiliation by the foreign imperialists. Troops were also dispatched to Tibet during this time after the Tibetans rebelled against the consolidation of Chinese rule. Meanwhile, the CCP consolidated their power within the country by authorizing police action against political adversaries, anti-communists, bandits, and groups of people who opposed the CCP's political dominance.

After experimenting with land reform in Jianggang and Jianxi, Mao finally had the opportunity to enforce it across the entire nation. The Agrarian Reform Law of 1950 effectively destroyed the feudal and semi-feudal class being confiscating their land and redistributing it to the peasants. Land was also seized from foreign ownership, severely diminishing the power of numerous private industrialists. Despite these radical measures, the CCP was able to propel economic growth by reducing urban inflation, creating a more disciplined labor force, and securing the confidence of the capitalists (who surprisingly began to see communist rule as being "good for business"). The introduction of a marriage law and trade-union law also helped to solidify the CCP's reputation for bringing bold reforms to the nation.

The early years of the People's Republic of China were nevertheless not free from conflict and strife. The Suppression of Counterrevolutionaries campaign inflicted violence on the KMT former leaders, the heads of secret societies, religious, and religious authorities. The Three-Antis campaign decimated the communists who had been perceived as fraternizing too closely with the nation's capitalists. The capitalists themselves were subjected to The Five-Antis campaign, which compelled obedience to the CCP via charges of tax evasion, bribery, theft of state property and dishonesty when entering into contractual obligations with the government contracts. University professors were not spared either. Mao had benefited from access to the Western liberal tradition, but the new generation would be exposed only to Soviet intellectual discourse.

In 1953, Mao launched his First Five-Year Plan[lii] to promote the nation's rapid industrialization. This plan was based on the Soviet experience; the CCP benefited from financial assistance and technical expertise on how to plan and execute ambitious goals while remaining true to Stalinist economic priorities. Over eighty percent of China's population lived in the rural areas, but the CCP government invested over eighty percent of its budget into the urban economy. Heavy industry was significantly promoted over agriculture, which was mostly undeveloped. The CCP began promoting voluntary forms of agricultural collectivization in the rural areas, ushering in the development of small collectives that consisted of between 20-30 households. Tensions developed between the land-owning peasants (who were forced to surrender the land they owned to the collectives without any financial benefits) and the landless peasants (who were more receptive to the collectivistic model). Many also resisted the central government's policies of extracting agricultural surpluses from the countryside to pay for the nation's investments in capital equipment, and to feed a growing urban population.

In the urban centers of industry and commerce, the capitalists and private merchants were pressured to form combined their individually-owned enterprises with the state. This was part of Mao's plan to engender a "socialist transformation" of China's industries and businesses. After facing the terror of the Five-Antis campaign, many capitalists were willing to cooperate with the government to resume the operation of their businesses. In any case, the government had gained monopoly control over the banking sector that the capitalists were compelled to rely on the government to keep making profits. As the nation's agriculture, commerce, and industry underwent a socialist transformation, its urban population grew from 77 million in 1953 to 99.5 million in 1957.

This pattern of migration created a problem for the CCP. The nation's agricultural sector was not developing fast enough to generate the surplus capital needed to feed the increasing number of workers in the urban centers, or to be reinvested to modernize farming methods further. This would contribute to the disastrous food shortages of the

Great Leap Forward. The financial assistance provided by the Soviet Union also had to be paid back. Finally, the development of the nation's economy required the participation of individuals with technical expertise (i.e. the nation's intelligentsia). Unlike the peasants and the capitalists, the intellectuals were not readily brought into the party line.

When Mao introduced the "Hundred Flowers" campaign[liii] in 1956 ("Let a hundred flowers blossom, a hundred schools of thought contend," the objective was help convert the nation's intellectuals to communism. Instead, they began to critique the principles of communism, the CCP, and the Chinese government. They would pay dearly for openly voicing their dissent when Mao retaliated with a vicious anti-rightist campaign.

Chapter 10 – The Great Leap Forward

In 1958, Mao initiated his second Five Year Plan (1958 - 1963) to modernize China's agriculture and industries and allow it to catch up with its American counterpart[liv]. This plan, which was named the Great Leap Forward, aimed to leapfrog the more typical process of industrialization, where businesses slowly accumulated the capital needed to invest in expensive and sophisticated machinery that would improve on efficiency and production rates. Unlike the Soviet Union, however, China had a denser population and no surplus of agricultural produce that could be converted into capital. Mao decided that China should industrialize rapidly by tapping into the sheer size of its labor force and eschew the traditional reliance on machine-centered industrial processes.

That year, an experimental commune[lv] was established in the north-central province of Henan. Each commune would house approximately 5,000 families that owned no private property, tools, or livestock. Everything was owned and managed by the commune. It provided members with food, schools, entertainment, nurseries for the young, healthcare, and "retirement homes" for the elderly who could no longer work. Each sub-division oversaw specific duties and tasks. Soldiers worked alongside the people, while CCP members ensured all decisions made were compliant with the party's ideology. The goal was to ultimately accelerate the development of China's agriculture and industries through this form of centralized economic planning. When 1958 ended, the CCP had successfully placed 700 million people into 26,578 communes across the nation.

The major problem with the commune system was that political beliefs and a dogmatic insistence on ideological purity triumphed over common sense and working expertise. Everyone was zealously encouraged to exceed the targets that had been set for them through the use of sheer hard work and determination. This zeal is most evident in the establishment of development of small backyard steel furnaces in every village and urban neighborhood, which collectively contributed to the nation's annual steel production. At the very beginning, the Great Leap Forward campaign seemed to be working. Major increases in the production of steel, coal, grain, cotton, timber, and cement were recorded. The quality of the steel produced in such conditions, however, was dubious.

By the following year, the catastrophic failure of the Great Leap Forward was evident. The farm machinery that had been produced haphazardly fell apart when they were used. The low-quality steel that was used to construct new buildings ensured they did not hold up for long. (The steel that had been produced by all the backyard furnaces across the nation were too substandard to even be used for construction). Overworked and suffering from insufficient sleep, thousands of workers were injured while working. These technical and managerial oversights were compounded by the Soviet Union withdrawing financial support for China, as well as three consecutive years of natural disasters. After excellent weather conditions in 1958, the nation suffered floods and droughts in the following years.

The diversion of a significant section of the workforce to small-scale industrial production and the inefficiency of the commune system with regards to agricultural production meant there was an insufficient surplus of food to make up for food shortage caused by the three years of natural disasters. The estimates for the exact number of Chinese citizens who died because of the disastrous The Great Leap Forward vary, but a 2010 estimate based on recently declassified documents placed the total death count at a staggering 45 million people[lvi].

Starvation, malnutrition, and illness claimed the majority of the lives lost during the Great Famine of 1958 to 1962. Between 2 to 3 million of those who died lost their lives to relatively trivial infractions. When commune leaders argued with CCP officials that the goals set for their commune were impossible, they would be charged with being a "bourgeois reactionary" and imprisoned. Regular workers who were suspected of being ideological traitors, or of simply not working hard enough, could be beaten, hung, or drowned in ponds. Other punishments included being forced to eat feces and being mutilated. When food was rationed during the famine, starvation became a common form of punishment.

Mao himself was comfortably ensconced in Zhongnanhai, Beijing. How did he react to reports of millions of Chinese people starving to death (with some resorting to cannibalism) in the countryside? In March 1959, he ordered CCP officials to take ownership of up to one-third of all the grain available, a greater portion than ever before. Meeting minutes indicate that he was indifferent to their suffering: "When there is not enough to eat people starve to death. It is better to let half of the people die so that the other half can eat their fill[lvii]."

He had to admit the program had been a horrendous failure. He did not readily accept the blame for its shortcomings, however. Given his popularity with the masses, Mao could not be easily displaced. He remained the Chairman of the CCP but resigned from his position as Head of State. Liu Shaoqi, Zhou Enlai, and Deng Xiaoping stepped in to govern the nation, and they decided to abandon the Great Leap Forward in 1960. The communes were reduced to a smaller size, private ownership of the land was reintroduced, and peasants were incentivized by the possibility selling any surplus food they produced.

Meanwhile, an internal division brewed within the CCP. One division believed that the Great Leap forward failed because of implementation (i.e. bureaucratic failures and mismanagement), while the other group opined that China needed to place a higher priority on technical expertise and material incentives to spur the economy onward.

Chapter 11 – The Cultural Revolution

Mao was not content with the prospect of losing political power and control in the Chinese government, or with the possibility of being reduced to a symbolic figurehead. The nation's alliance with the Soviet Union had also deteriorated. Mao witnessed Stalin's denunciation by Nikita Khrushchev in 1956, as well as Khrushchev's removal from power in 1964. When he saw Wu Han's play "Hai Rui Dismissed from Office[lviii]" – which featured a Ming dynasty official who dared to criticize the emperor – he interpreted it as a coded means of undermining his authority and proclaiming support for defense minister Peng Dehuai[lix], who had been dismissed after openly confronting Mao about the failures of The Great Leap Forward at the 1959 Lushan Conference[lx].

He was also concerned that "bourgeois" elements were gaining influence within the CCP, government, and society at large. Everything was at stake: his influence, power, and position within the party and the legacy of his vision of communism in the country. The Cultural Revolution[lxi] was presented as a nation-wide means of purging the nation of all "bourgeois" and "reactionary" elements, who were labelled as "class enemies" and traitors to communist ideals.

In 1965, Wu Han's play was investigated, publicly denounced and banned for its "reactionary" political nature. This would establish a precedent for the radicalization of all art forms under the Cultural Revolution, effectively censoring all forms of expression – music, cinema, plays, fiction, nonfiction, poetry, visual arts – and replacing them with pro-Mao propaganda. Mao formally detailed his concerns about "bourgeois" infiltrators in a CCP Central Committee document on May 16, 1966. In August that year, the Cultural Revolution was launched across the nation at the Eleventh Plenum of the Eighth Central Committee.

The Cultural Revolution was a grand bid to secure power for Mao and his supporters within the CCP, but it also had widespread effects across the entire Chinese society. Mao had the support of radicalized youths (who formed the feared "Red Guards[lxii]") that hung on fervently to his rhetoric, and they were ready to inflict violence on anyone deemed to be a traitor to his ideals. Nothing was sacred or spared, as the Red Guards have been urged to annihilate the "four olds" wherever they encountered them: old ideas, customs, habits, and culture[lxiii]. Red Guard divisions were formed in university campuses and classrooms across the nation, and they took to the task of destroying their educational institutions, churches, shrines, shops, private homes, and libraries. On 5 August 1966, the first known death by torture occurred[lxiv]. The Red Guards kicked, trampled and poured boiling water over the headmistress of a prominent girls' school in Peking. She was made to transport heavy bricks as the Red Guards assaulted her with leather belts and wooden sticks embedded with nails. The Red Guards were not asked to curtail their violence when news of her death reached the CCP.

Mao had published his infamous "Little Red Book" (*Quotations from Chairman Mao Tse-tung*) in 1964 and wielded it as a massively influential propaganda tool across the nation. The Red Guards used his quotations to organize their ideals and actions, and it became the nation's undisputed bestseller as so many other local and foreign publications were banned for containing "reactionary" elements. The Little Red Book was ubiquitous in China throughout the Cultural Revolution. Its sales surpassed even that of the Bible during the 1960s, with over a billion copies printed. Mao was easily China's bestselling author for a decade, making millions while everyone else with riches to their name was suspect.

By 1967, the Red Guards and Mao loyalists had ousted many of the influential CCP leaders who had opposed or criticized Mao. Former President Liu Shaoqi[lxv] was expelled from the party in 1968. He died the following year after enduring brutal treatment during his arrest. Deng Xiaoping was also stripped of his power and position in the party, but he survived the Cultural Revolution and would eventually return to power after Mao's death. China's current president Xi Jinping's father, CCP veteran Xi Zhongxun, was also purged from the party, publicly humiliated and forced into exile during the Cultural Revolution.

By 1968, millions of urban youths (including a teenage Xi Jinping) were sent to the countryside to toil alongside the peasants. As older intellectuals, artisans, and professionals like doctors, lawyers and businessmen suffered verbal and physical abuse, the country's urban economy and industrial production was stifled by anarchy and chaos. The Red Guards had also begun to engage in rivalries and conflicts with one another, with each proclaiming themselves to be the singularly genuine adherent to Mao's ideals. Disillusioned with their inability to form a unified front, Mao sent most of them to toil in the countryside, restoring some semblance of order to the cities.

It is difficult to ascertain the exact number of lives lost during the Cultural Revolution, but a 2011 estimate places the number of people who died during this period to fall somewhere between 500, 000 to 8 million[lxvi]. Tens of millions of people, however, were estimated to have been persecuted and harassed during this turbulent period. Economic output was curtailed, but the nation also suffered cultural losses that cannot be quantified. The nation's rich tradition of literature and fine arts that had been cultivated over centuries were dismissed overnight as being feudalistic, bourgeois, revisionist and imperialistic. Mao Yu Run, a professor of music who lived through the Cultural Revolution, recalls the inescapable cult of personality that Mao propagated throughout the nation during this period:

"From then on, in a country of one billion people, we could only hear two voices, the voice of Mao, that hovered in our territorial sky of 9,600,000 square kilometers, and the voice of one billion people singing in unison the hymn praising Mao: "Mao, dear Mao. I march on where ever your big hand points; I do whatever I am told; I am a tamed instrument of the Party[lxvii]."

The Cultural Revolution would finally end with Mao's death on September 9, 1976, at the age of 82[lxviii]. By now, the population at large had become disillusioned with his ideals and the leadership of the CCP. Despite all the propaganda, they could see these principles and philosophies were a smokescreen for the blatant power plays that were occurring within the party lines. Even then, Mao's image was too central to the CCP for his successors to tarnish it. The Gang of Four - Mao's third wife Jiang Qing[lxix], Wang Hongwen, Zhang Chunqiao, and Yao Wenyuan – were publicly blamed for all the losses suffered during the Cultural Revolution and were purged from the party. Deng Xiaoping would return to power after Mao's death and implement many economic reforms that aimed to repair the damage inflicted by the misguided policies of the era. It would take decades to repair the nation's educational system, and the individuals who had their schooling disrupted by the radical revolutionary fervor of the time became a "lost generation," unable to find their footing in the era of pragmatic economic growth that Deng spearheaded[lxx].

Chapter 12 – What Did Maoism Stand For?

Frank Dikötter, a Dutch historian with a specialization in modern China, has argued that the tumultuous decades of the Great Leap Forward and Cultural Revolution effectively erased the faith that the Chinese population once had in Mao's ideals: "Even before Mao died, people buried Maoism[lxxi]."

Mao's image may remain in China, but the calamities it faced during his life would ironically engender an acceptance of the market reforms that Deng Xiaoping introduced. But what is Maoism? Mao was informed by Marx and Lenin's ideas, as well as the model of communism the Soviets adopted. He nevertheless believed that it was the rural peasantry that would form the revolutionary masses, instead of the urban workers[lxxii]. Maoism placed more importance on the peasant masses and viewed urban industrialization with much distrust. From his perspectives, the industrialists were also prone to be swayed by the kind of bourgeois elitism he despised. This ideal is best embodied by the backyard furnaces that were ubiquitous during The Great Leap Forward. Maoism also holds that a socialist population is always under threat from the re-emergence of bourgeois values and must be continuously re-educated and purged to retain socialist purity.

After Mao's death, Maoism would inspire revolutionaries in other nations with sizable rural populations and a history of imperial exploitation. The Nepalese rebels and the Naxalites in India are arguably the last descendants of Maoism. The Khmer Rouge is perhaps the most notorious proponents of Maoism, having killed 1.7 million Cambodians during the anti-urban purges in the 1970s.

Mao's teachings influenced revolutionaries in several nations with large rural populations, but the Nepalese insurgency is perhaps the last Maoist movement left. The "ultra-Maoist" Khmer Rouge, whose anti-urban purges in the 1970s left at least 1.7 million Cambodians dead, has essentially disappeared. And save for one tiny faction, Peru's Maoist Shining Path has dissolved since the arrest of its founder, Abimael Guzman (aka "President Gonzalo"), in 1992.

Was Mao himself a true Maoist? Jung Chang, a Chinese-born British writer whose international bestseller *Wild Swans* (1952) is banned in China, has argued that Mao did not abide by the tenets of hard work, frugality, and abstinence that he forced on the entire population after he rose to power. Mao presented himself with simplicity in terms of clothes (i.e. the ubiquitous Mao suit), but Chang notes that he indulged in a gourmet's diet, had no less than 50 estates to his name, and was regularly entertained by young girls and courtesans. Li Zhisui, Mao's private physician from 1955 to 1976, supported Chang's description of Mao as a decadent tyrant in his memoir *The Private Life of Chairman Mao* (1988).

Conclusion

It is difficult to arrive at a definitive evaluation of Mao's legacy in China due to his long career and the sheer scale of his successes and failures. Mao's legacy as a shrewd military tactician cannot be denied: it was his guerrilla warfare tactics that allowed the CCP to survive the Nationalists and eventually defeat them. After decades of humiliation and exploitation by foreign and local oppressors, the Chinese people turned to Mao for his ability to restore pride, dignity, and confidence in the strength of the Chinese society.

If Mao had resigned from power and influence shortly after announcing the formation of the People's Republic of China, he would have retired as a national hero. His insistence on remaining in power for as long as he could, however, left him with a tainted legacy. As an administrator of the nation, he did successfully attempt to halt the excesses and inefficiencies of the bureaucracy, promote self-reliance within the people and promote the nation's industrialization. His revolutionary zest was nevertheless less suited to governing the nation. Even now, it is hard for people to gain a tangible sense of the sheer trauma and millions of deaths that were lost during the Great Leap Forward and the Cultural Revolution. Mao's own body is preserved for perpetuity, but there are no monuments, memorials or sculptures to commemorate the millions of Chinese citizens who starved to death or those who were murdered upon accusations of being "bourgeois" or "reactionary."

How do we judge Mao as a person? His physician Li Zishui described him as "a merciless tyrant who crushed anybody who disobeyed him[lxxiii]." Mao's sheer will to power was undoubtedly unquestionable.

How else would the son of a peasant rise through the ranks of the Chinese Communist Party to become its most indispensable symbol? He certainly earned many opponents and adversaries within the CCP, but his ability to build loyal alliances with powerful party members and the Russians ensured that he returned to power after being repeatedly ousted. This was a man who established a cult of personality over the largest population in the world (one-quarter of the world' population) for several decades – the thought of purging Mao from China appears unthinkable.

Dr. Li has also raised the possibility that Mao was not genuinely capable of love, friendship or warmth for others. Dr. Li notes that Mao had announced, during a 1957 speech in Moscow, that he was willing to lose half of China's population (300 million people). When millions of his countrymen did start starving to death during the famine, his evident lack of empathy and concern mirrored his earlier proclamations. Erstwhile allies and followers were similarly disposed or abandoned once they had become disillusioned with the man behind the myth.

With Mao, it is also essential to make a distinction between the words and the deeds. Mao is famed for his emphasis on gender equality via his statement "Women hold up half the sky." Mao's policies encouraged women to participate in political life, in the fields, and in the factories. In the propaganda of the era, women were presented as "iron women" who performed "masculine" labor at the steel furnaces while ensuring their domestic responsibilities were well taken care of. There were nevertheless glass ceilings: no woman has ever been appointed to the Politburo standing committee[lxxiv].Similar glass ceilings existed in the urban workplaces and rural areas where women struggled to fulfill both their professional and domestic responsibilities[lxxv]. Mao himself did not treat his wives as true equals and was never faithful to any of them.

It is difficult to reduce Mao to the figure of a monster or a hero. One could make the case that he was a severely flawed person who made indispensable contributions to the nation. Even if they disagree with his policies and their outcomes, some look to his anti-elitism and emphasis of equality as an important ideal in today's income-stratified society. Others dismiss any notion of Mao as being benevolent or well-intentioned, arguing that he is the most Machiavellian leader of the twentieth century, who hypocritically wielded ideologies and policies for the sake of consolidating and perpetuating his power[lxxvi]. In any case, China's present ruler Xi Jinping has proclaimed that a total denunciation of Mao would cause chaos and strip the CCP of its legitimacy. As Mao's old enemy class – the intelligentsia – adopt an increasingly negative view of his actions, the state-owned media attempt to defend him. Mao's portraits may be absent from official CCP functions and meetings, but it will take a drastic development or a long time before China can disown his legacy.

Preview of Alexander Hamilton A Captivating Guide to one of the Founding Fathers of the United States of America

Introduction

An Extraordinary Immigrant

ALEXANDER HAMILTON is one of the most extraordinary figures in American history. A deep thinker, a military leader, and a political dynamo, he was George Washington's right-hand man and perhaps the most important figure in the shaping of the Constitution. His policies and practices in government set the United States down a path of commercial wealth and economic stability. His ideas still resonate in the powerful nation he helped create.

During his time, Hamilton was a divisive figure. A political extremist who antagonized the conservative parts of the new republic while protecting its former opponents. The man at the heart of the nation's first major sex scandal. A political operator whose actions outraged opponents and eventually led to the duel that cost him his life.

It was an extraordinary life, made more extraordinary by Hamilton's origins. He was an outsider, an immigrant from the Caribbean who arrived in New York to make a new life for himself. In doing so, he helped to shape the framework of politics and commerce in America. In retrospect, the amazing thing about his fame is not its recent resurgence, but that it took so long for him to be widely recognized.

This is the story of Alexander Hamilton. The story of a nation born in blood, in struggle, and in the dynamism that immigrants could bring.

Chapter 1: Early Years

A Caribbean Childhood

ALEXANDER HAMILTON was born on the island of Nevis in the British West Indies. This jungle-swathed island, dominated by its towering central mountain, lay at the heart of British commercial interests in the latter half of the 18th century. The growing popularity of sugar, both for cooking and for hot drinks, made the Caribbean sugarcane fields a vast source of wealth for Britain - greater than all the combined efforts of the North American colonies. "White gold," as some labelled the sugar, was one of the most important commodities in the world.

This made a deeply divided and often unpleasant society. Most of Nevis' inhabitants were either slaves imported to work the sugarcane fields or lowlifes shipped in from London to work as servants and overseers – criminals sent abroad as much to clean up the capital's streets as to help in Nevis. A small elite of plantation aristocrats oversaw them, with an insecure middle class providing a buffer between the wealthy in their mansions and the rabble in the streets.

Hamilton's parents grew up in the middle class. The bright and beautiful Rachel Faucette came from a family that owned a small, struggling plantation. In 1750, she fled an unpleasant marriage to an older man named Johann Michael Lavien. In the aftermath, she met and fell in love with James Hamilton.

James was a Scottish noble. As the fourth son of a large family, he was never likely to inherit wealth and instead had to find his way in the world. But he showed none of the drive and acumen that led his brothers to flourish, and instead found himself in a series of financial difficulties. After a dispiriting apprenticeship in the linen trade, he decided in 1741 to travel to the West Indies and seek his fortune in white gold. Amiable but lazy and not skilled in commerce, his attempt to break into the sugar trade on St. Kitts led to financial difficulties, from which he had to be rescued by family and friends. By 1748, his dream of an exotic fortune had collapsed, and he was working as a port official.

Divorces were hard to obtain and brought with them a huge social stigma. Even when Rachel's husband eventually divorced her, the settlement banned her from future marriage. So, Rachel and James settled down together outside the legal and social protection of wedlock. They lived the life of a married couple and even shared Hamilton's surname, but they were not married in the eyes of the law. Together, they had two children - James Junior and Alexander.

Alexander Hamilton's date of birth is uncertain. He would later claim it was 1757, but earlier evidence indicates a date of January the 11th 1755.

The young Hamilton was thin and frail, with reddish-brown hair that spoke to his Scottish ancestry. He grew up in a waterfront property his mother had inherited in Charlestown, the capital of Nevis. He was home-schooled by an elderly Jewish woman and possibly by his mother, who was of French ancestry, resulting in a fluency in French.

It was on Nevis that Hamilton developed his fascination with dueling. The island was a dramatic place, lying at the center of the skirmishes between English, French, and Spanish ships for control of the Caribbean. Privateers and pirates were common and sometimes came ashore to duel. But the respectable side of island society also had a fondness for dueling, as a way of protecting aristocratic honor.

The island also shaped his views on slavery. Most of the population were slaves, and he bore witness to their short lives and cruel treatment.

Nevis was a strange and exciting place for a boy to grow up, one that fostered Hamilton's sense of drama and romance.

In 1765, the Hamilton's relocated to Christiansted on St. Croix, where James had business. There, Rachel was faced with the social stigma of having left her previous husband. The illegitimacy of the Hamilton children was laid bare. Worse yet, James abandoned his wife and family, leading to an enduring sense of distance between Alexander Hamilton and his father.

Strong-willed and independent, Rachel was not to be undone by James' departure. Unusually for a woman in 18th-century St. Croix, she established her own business, selling food to planters. She also made money hiring out five slaves she inherited from her mother. Some of this money went into providing books for her sons to read. They included Machiavelli and Plutarch as well as poetry and sermons. Whatever Rachel's own education, she knew what was held in high regard at the time and led her son down the intellectual path followed by the 18th century's enlightened intelligentsia.

In February 1768, both Rachel and Alexander fell ill with a terrible fever. He survived, but his mother succumbed to the illness on the 19th.

The Hamilton boys became orphans, dependent upon the community. But their suffering was far from over.

Finding Work

A LEGAL BATTLE BROKE out over Rachel's estate. Johann Michael Lavien insisted that the property should go to Peter, the child of their marriage. After a year of uncertainty, Peter was awarded the estate. The Hamilton boys were disinherited, left with none of their mother's small wealth.

The boys' new guardian was their 32-year-old cousin Peter Lytton, a failed businessman in the mold of their father. In July 1769, Lytton committed suicide, leaving no money to the boys. The 16-year-old James and 14-year-old Alexander were left alone in the world.

The two boys pursued different paths. James became a carpenter's apprentice, living with his master and learning a craft. Alexander was taken in by the merchant Thomas Stevens and his wife, Ann. He lived with them and their five children in a fine house full of respectable people. Edward Stevens, who was a year older than Hamilton, became his closest friend. Similarities between Edward and Hamilton, along with the way the Stevens family took the young man in, have led to much speculation that Hamilton was the son of Thomas Stevens, not James Hamilton. This fits with other facts about Hamilton and his mother, including Lavien's accusations of adultery against Rachel and Hamilton's distant relationships with his brother and legal father. But there is no solid evidence and so it is unlikely to ever be more than plausible speculation.

Alexander Hamilton's improved social status complemented his employment. He found work fitting his inquisitive intellect, as a clerk for the New York-based trading house of Beekman and Cruger. They had been a supplier for his mother's business and dealt in everything planters needed, from bricks to mules to dried food.

This was a busy environment which suited Hamilton's active mind. He learned to keep track of freight, chart ships' courses, and calculate prices in the many different currencies flowing in from Europe. He also learned lessons that would form his future career in politics and government, such as the importance of cash supplies in maintaining trade, the ways that smugglers and merchants worked, and the dangers of relying on a single export.

Hamilton was embittered by his lowly standing in a class-conscious society and determined to better himself. While other young men in the trade houses frittered away their time and money on high living, Hamilton focused on his work because he was determined to rise above his station in life.

Working for Beekman and Cruger exposed Hamilton to the burgeoning mercantile elite of New York. Family trading firms of this type often sent younger members from New York to the Caribbean to serve as their agents, and Nicholas Cruger was one of them. Through Cruger and his peers, Hamilton began to learn about the bustling trade city that would one day become his home.

In 1769, one of the partners retired and Beekman and Cruger became Kortright and Cruger. Two years later, ill health forced Nicholas Cruger to return to New York, leaving Hamilton in charge of the firm's business in St. Croix for five months. He flourished in this leadership role, vigorously pursuing debts, advising on how to get a cargo safely through hostile waters, and even reprimanding an older captain who disappointed him.

From 1771, Hamilton, like all young men on the island, was obliged to attend monthly militia drills. This first taste of military experience was designed to prepare him to deal with slave uprisings, which were a constant threat in a society built on cruelly oppressing most of the population.

Around the same time, his written works were published for the first time, his youthful poems seeing light in the Royal Danish American Gazette. These were followed into the paper in the fall of 1772 by a letter he had written describing a devastating storm that tore through the islands. The letter impressed readers, and local businessmen set up a fund to send Hamilton to North America to be educated.

Late that year or early the next, Alexander Hamilton set sail for Boston, never to return to his Caribbean home.

Education

THANKS TO THE FUNDS he had been given and introductory letters from a minister in St. Croix, Hamilton soon found his feet on the colonial mainland, a land of diverse settlers under British rule. He took up a place studying at Elizabethtown Academy, where he filled the gaps in his education that would prevent him from attending college. There he learned Latin, Greek, and advanced mathematics. Again, he worked hard, taking extensive notes and pacing the grounds while he recited and memorized lessons.

In Elizabethtown, Hamilton's charm and intelligence allowed him to build a network of social connections far beyond those available in St. Croix. These included William Livingston, a wealthy lawyer and one of the biggest influences on this part of Hamilton's life. Livingston and many of those around him were Whigs, followers of a political tradition that called for civil liberties and the curbing of royal power by parliament. The Presbyterian Livingston's home was a hotbed of religious and political dissent, but also of glamour. Hamilton befriended Livingston's children, young men and women of around his own age, through whom he may have had his first encounters with Aaron Burr, a friend of Brockholst Livingston.

Other new acquaintances included William Alexander, known as Lord Stirling, an aristocrat with a lavish lifestyle and rebellious leanings, and Elias Boudinot, a lawyer, mine owner, and future member of the Continental Congress. Such men shaped Hamilton's political outlook even as they expanded his social horizons. They were reformers who sought a closer relationship between the colonies and Britain but who would become revolutionaries when the call for reform failed.

Within six months, Hamilton moved on to college. He first applied to Princeton, a center of Presbyterian and Whig feeling with which his friends had strong ties. But while he impressed his interviewer, the college would not let the impatient Hamilton follow the accelerated program of learning he sought.

Instead, Hamilton went to King's College in New York, where Lord Stirling sat on the board. King's College was a more conservative place, many of its staff Tories, the arch-conservatives who supported traditional monarchic British rule. But New York was a place deeply divided and as the revolution approached it would be torn apart by conflict between Tories and Whigs. Not only would Hamilton be exposed to the greatest commercial center in the new world, he would also be thrust into a radicalizing political debate that pushed young men toward allegiance to a side. Under its president, Dr. Miles Cooper, King's was a strict center of conservatism where carousing and rabble-rousing were not tolerated, but which sat adjacent to a red-light district and radical gathering spot. The contrasts of pre-revolutionary New York could not have been more clearly displayed to Hamilton.

Having entered formal education later than his peers, Hamilton worked hard to race through his studies and make up for lost time. He attended private tutorials, audited lectures, and read the books made available to him, filling his mind with literature, rhetoric, philosophy, science, and everything else the curriculum had to offer. At first, he aimed to be a doctor and so attended the anatomy lectures of pioneering surgeon Dr. Samuel Clossy. Diligent in his work, he set aside time for morning walks and leisure but avoided the pranks that saw other students' names recorded in Dr. Cooper's Black Book.

Hamilton and Robert Troup, his friend and roommate, formed a club to practice speaking, writing, and debating skills, a club that included his old friend Edward Stevens. There, Hamilton sharpened the rhetorical skills that would serve him so well in the aftermath of the revolution. He also refined his radical views, writing anti-British pamphlets as he became increasingly staunch in his reforming opinions. His first published piece on politics was a defense of the Boston Tea Party in 1773, in which he used his specialist knowledge of commerce as well as his education in politics.

New York was the perfect home for a young man looking to find his place in the world. Over a dozen languages were spoken in this cosmopolitan city filled with traders and colonists from across Europe. It was also ideal for someone invested in political debate. In April 1774, New York had its own tea party protest, even as the British authorities mobilized to clamp down on dissent in the colonies. The causes behind the rebellion were complex, but commerce played a central part. How and where taxes should be raised, how the interests of government and business should be balanced, how those voices were to be heard - all came together in triggering a great revolt.

On the 6th of July 1774, Hamilton made his first public speech, at a radical meeting in New York. He spoke mesmerizingly of liberty, justice, and freedom. It was a speech that made this astonishing young man a hero of the radical cause in conservative New York. He went on to become one of the city's foremost pamphleteers, writing anonymously published tracts while boycotts and conventions turned dissent into the specter of war. His style was eloquent, forthright, and aggressive - the perfect voice for an increasingly angry opposition.

Chapter 2: Revolutionary

Into the Militias

ON THE NIGHT OF THE 18th of April 1775, a skirmish broke out at Lexington between a battalion of revolutionary farmers known as the Minutemen and a force of British troops. The British had already declared Massachusetts in rebellion, but now war had arrived.

In New York, the news was greeted with exuberant marches by radicals, while Tories hid away in fear of violence. The Sons of Liberty emptied the City Hall arsenal and British supply ships, equipping themselves with thousands of weapons.

Militias swiftly assembled and began training for war. One was formed at King's College, despite Dr. Cooper's staunch opposition to the war. Under the command of Edward Fleming, a former officer in an English regiment, young men including Hamilton and Troup marched back and forth in the green jackets and red heart badges of a company known as the Corsicans. As always, Hamilton was an enthusiastic learner, studying tactics and gunnery between the daily drills.

During this period, Hamilton also demonstrated the moderating, merciful tendency he would display in the aftermath of the war. When, on the night of the 10th of May, an armed mob came to seize the despised Dr. Cooper, Hamilton leaped to his teacher's defense. Standing before the mob in the grounds of the college, he employed his rhetorical skills to delay the angry crowd, giving Cooper the time he needed to escape. Despite their violently opposing views, Hamilton did not want to see a man he knew lynched. It was an approach he demonstrated again later in the year when he defended the Tory printer James Rivington as patriots put him out of business.

In his political pamphlets, Hamilton had foreseen the shape of the war - one to be won through irregular tactics and skirmishes rather than traditional pitched battles and in which France and Spain would back the revolutionary side.

On the 15th of June, the Second Continental Congress appointed George Washington to lead the revolutionary armies. Two days later, in the first pitch battle of the war, the rebels inflicted heavy casualties on the British. Not only had war come, but it seemed it could be won.

On the night of the 23rd of August, Hamilton took part in his first military action, retrieving artillery from Fort George under fire from the British warship HMS Asia. But most of his rebellious activity for the first year came in print, as he continued to write poems, journalism, and political tracts.

In February 1776, Hamilton left his studies behind to become a captain in a newly raised artillery company. He was offered the rank of brigade major as military aide to Lord Stirling but preferred active service to a role as a commander's subordinate.

As an officer, Hamilton was popular with his men. He shared their hardships and suffering. Dedicated to equality, he lobbied for his men to receive rations and pay equal to those of the Continental Army. Fastidious about dress and discipline, he drilled the men regularly and ensured they had smart matching uniforms. His dedication created a good impression among senior officers, winning him influential friends.

This early service was not all about display. Hamilton's troops played a part in constructing New York's defenses, and he led them in a nighttime raid against Sandy Hook lighthouse.

On the 4th of July 1776, the colonies declared independence from England. In response, New York, already besieged by British forces, suffered heavy bombardments. Hamilton's company was among those returning fire. In the process, one of his cannons was mishandled and exploded, killing several of his men. He directly faced the grim danger and loss of war.

This defensive work was to no avail. Patriot forces in New York were vastly outnumbered, and Washington was forced to withdraw. Hamilton served in the rear guard of this well-executed retreat, losing his heavy guns in the process.

After the fall of New York, Hamilton's company came under Washington's command. The general saw Hamilton building defenses on Harlem Heights and then commanding in battle at White Plains. As the demoralized rebels were forced back by the British, Washington was forced to resort to the way of fighting Hamilton had predicted - skirmishing and irregular warfare. Despite ill health, Hamilton commanded his artillery in covering their retreat and then launching counterattacks. His leadership at Trenton and Princeton, as Washington reversed the tide of war, won Hamilton praise even as Patriot spirits rose.

Washington's Aide

HAMILTON HAD RESISTED previous invitations to join the staff of generals. But when Washington came calling in January 1777, he finally accepted. On the 1st of March, he officially joined the general's staff and was promoted to lieutenant colonel.

Hamilton took his place on Washington's staff with his usual enthusiasm, and efficiency. The general provided the volatile young man with a mentor's steadying hand, while Hamilton brought bureaucratic efficiency as well as political and economic depth to Washington's leadership group. Their personalities sometimes clashed, and they developed a partnership based more on mutual admiration than affection. But it was one of the most fruitful partnerships in political history.

Washington struggled to express himself, and so the eloquent Hamilton found his place drafting the commander's correspondence. Soon, he had access to all the confidential information of the military headquarters and was issuing orders on Washington's behalf. He also offered advice to the general, who famously lost many battles on the way to winning the war. When the French entered the conflict, Hamilton became a fluent translator between their officers and Washington. While his official position remained unchanged, his duties evolved from private secretary to something similar to a chief of staff, dealing with diplomacy, intelligence, and the management of senior officers. This broadened his political and economic education. It also taught him to despise the small-minded concerns of local interests, as he and Washington struggled to hold American resources together in service to the collective good.

Among Washington's aides, Hamilton found a close sense of family his life had been missing, including the closest friendship of his life with John Laurens and a close bond with the glamorous French nobleman the Marquis de Lafayette. In the meritocratic revolutionary army, he found the opportunity for the advancement he had always sought, and in dealing with leading men across the colonies, he found a network of contacts that would serve him well in his future career. Not all this contact with great men was good for Hamilton. His cutting eloquence made him the bane of those he disagreed with. The extraordinary power Washington sometimes delegated to him, including authorization to demand troops from senior commanders, was bound to aggravate the more stubborn and self-important of the senior men leading the revolution. Nevertheless, these four years with Washington were the making of Hamilton.

Service with Washington brought Hamilton onto the field of battle again. In 1778, at the Battle of Monmouth, he played a critical part in turning around an army that threatened to collapse. During the fighting, he was injured when his horse was shot.

In the aftermath of the battle, he testified in the court-martial of General Charles Lee for his failings there. Lee was found guilty, and Hamilton earned the acrimony of many of Lee's supporters, including Aaron Burr.

The bad blood between Washington's supporters and those of Lee also led to Hamilton's first involvement in a duel. On the 23rd of December 1778, Hamilton's friend Laurens dueled Lee over disparaging comments the former general made about Washington. Hamilton, Laurens's second, bore witness to Lee's wounding and Laurens's victory. Honor had been served in what, to those involved, seemed a gentlemanly fashion.

Social occasions organized by the wives and daughters of senior officers gave Hamilton a chance to meet eligible young women. He showed an interest in several women before, in February 1780, he began courting Elizabeth Schuyler, known as Eliza. She was smart, good-looking, and the daughter of a wealthy Patriot family - everything he was looking for in a wife. Hamilton was smitten by Eliza, and the relationship moved fast. That March, the couple decided they would marry.

The wedding took place at the Schuyler mansion in Albany on the 14th of December 1780. The small ceremony in the family home was in keeping with the culture of the Dutch settlers from whom the Schuylers descended. It was made even smaller by the lack of guests on Hamilton's side. He had no family in attendance, despite writing to invite his father. Of his friends on Washington's staff, only one, James McHenry, could spare the time to attend the wedding. Hamilton's small support network consisted of men heavily engaged in the war.

Field Command

HAMILTON'S MARRIAGE brought him great happiness, but setbacks in his career tainted it. Congress had passed over him in selecting men for diplomatic appointments. Washington, reliant on Hamilton's linguistic and writing skills, had refused him the chance to return to a field command. He felt frustrated at being held back from his desires and at serving as assistant, even if he was assistant to the Patriots' leading general.

In the middle of February 1781, tensions finally came to a head. A tense argument broke out between Hamilton and Washington. The more senior man tried to repair the breach, but Hamilton was determined to move on. His temper triggered the argument, and his pride would not allow him to let it go, even after Washington offered to make amends. After a month of awkward but professional cooperation from both men, Hamilton left Washington's staff.

Temporarily out of service, Hamilton spent much of his time thinking and writing about government. He became convinced that a central national bank was needed to ensure the finances of the new nation and to defeat the British through a war of economic attrition. He also continued to develop his ideas about the political future of the nation, believing a strong central government was needed to ensure security and stability.

After repeatedly writing to Washington badgering him for a field command, Hamilton was finally granted his wish on the 31st of July 1781 - command of a battalion of light infantry from New York. In August, as Washington changed strategy from retaking New York city to besieging Yorktown, Hamilton left behind the pregnant Eliza to march to war.

After weeks of bombardment, on the night of the 14th of October, Washington ordered an assault against the British redoubts outside Yorktown. Hamilton was given command one of the two regiments making the night assault. He led his men in a bayonet charge on the British redoubt, capturing their target with few losses in ten minutes of swift action. During the assault, he hopped from the shoulder of a kneeling shoulder onto the enemy parapet, calling his men to follow. The decisive fight and Hamilton's bold part in it earned him a romantic reputation for death-defying courage.

The capture of the redoubts allowed the Americans to complete their siege line and within days the beleaguered British surrendered. The fall of Yorktown ensured American victory, though the war dragged on for another two years.

Having finally seen the action he craved, Hamilton would not participate in the rest of the war. Exhausted to the point of illness by years of hard work, he returned to his family and spent two months recovering. On the 22nd of January, Eliza gave birth to their son Philip, named after her father. Two months later, Hamilton gave up his military post, retaining his rank but giving up pay and a pension that his family would later come to miss.

The war had provided Hamilton with experience, contacts, and now a glamorous reputation. As America and Britain drifted towards peace, he would capitalise on this to find his place in the newly established nation.

Check out this book!

Primary and Secondary Sources

[i] Buruma, Ian. "Cult of the Chairman." March 2001. *The Guardian*. https://www.theguardian.com/world/2001/mar/07/china.features11. Accessed 10 February 2018.

[ii] "Deng Xiaoping." *Encyclopædia Britannica*. https://www.britannica.com/biography/Deng-Xiaoping. Accessed 10 February 2018.

[iii] Oakley, Barbara. *Evil Genes: Why Rome Fell, Hitler Rose, Enron Failed, and My Sister Stole My Mother's Boyfriend*. 2007.

[iv] Rummel, R. J. "The Holocaust in Comparative and Historical Perspective". *IDEA*. April 1998. http://www.ideajournal.com/articles.php?id=17. Accessed 10 February 2018.

[v] Kristof, Nicholas D. "Legacy of Mao Called 'Great Disaster." *The New York Times*. February 1989. http://www.nytimes.com/1989/02/07/world/legacy-of-mao-called-great-disaster.html. Accessed 10 February 2018.

[vi] Pantsov, Alexander and Levine, Steven I. *Mao: The Real Story*. 2012.

[vii] Ibid.

[viii] Chang, Jung and Halliday, Jon. *Mao: The Unknown Story*. 2005.

[ix] Snow, Edgar. *Red Star over China*. 1937.

[x] Pantsov, Alexander and Levine, Steven I. *Mao: The Real Story*. 2012.

[xi] Ibid.

xii Ibid.

xiii "Changsha." *Encyclopædia Britannica.* https://www.britannica.com/place/Changsha. Accessed 10 February 2018.

xiv "Sun Yat-sen." *Encyclopædia Britannica.* https://www.britannica.com/biography/Sun-Yat-sen. Accessed 10 February 2018.

xv Pantsov, Alexander and Levine, Steven I. *Mao: The Real Story.* 2012.

xvi Snow, Edgar. *Red Star over China.* 1937.

xvii Pantsov, Alexander and Levine, Steven I. *Mao: The Real Story.* 2012.

xviii Ibid.

xix Schram, Stuart Reynolds. *Mao's Road to Power vol. 1: Pre-Marxist Period, 1912-20.* 1992.

xx Pantsov, Alexander and Levine, Steven I. *Mao: The Real Story.* 2012.

xxi Ibid.

xxii "May Fourth Movement." *Encyclopædia Britannica.* https://www.britannica.com/event/May-Fourth-Movement. Accessed 10 February 2018

xxiii Schram, Stuart Reynolds. *Mao's Road to Power vol. 1: Pre-Marxist Period, 1912-20.* 1992.

xxiv "Russian Revolution of 1917." *Encyclopædia Britannica.* https://www.britannica.com/event/Russian-Revolution-of-1917. Accessed 10 February 2018.

xxv Chang, Jung and Halliday, Jon. *Mao: The Unknown Story.* 2005.

xxvi Pantsov, Alexander and Levine, Steven I. *Mao: The Real Story.* 2012.

xxvii Schram, Stuart Reynolds. *Mao's Road to Power vol. 1: Pre-Marxist Period, 1912-20.* 1992.

xxviii "Chinese Communist Party." *Encyclopædia Britannica.* https://www.britannica.com/topic/Chinese-Communist-Party. Accessed 10 February 2018.

xxix Ch'en, Kung-po. *The Communist Movement in China: An Essay Written in 1924.* 1966.

xxx "Nationalist Party." *Encyclopædia Britannica.* https://www.britannica.com/topic/Nationalist-Party-Chinese-political-party. Accessed 10 February 2018.

xxxi Pantsov, Alexander and Levine, Steven I. *Mao: The Real Story.* 2012.

xxxii Snow, Edgar. *Red Star over China.* 1937.

xxxiii Pantsov, Alexander and Levine, Steven I. *Mao: The Real Story.* 2012.

xxxiv "Three Principles of the People." *Encyclopædia Britannica.* https://www.britannica.com/event/Three-Principles-of-the-People. Accessed 10 February 2018.

xxxv Schram, Stuart Reynolds. *Mao's Road to Power vol. 2: National Revolution and Social Revolution, December 1920-June 1927.* 1992.

xxxvi Pantsov, Alexander and Levine, Steven I. *Mao: The Real Story.* 2012.

xxxvii "Chiang Kai-shek". *Encyclopædia Britannica.* https://www.britannica.com/biography/Chiang-Kai-shek. Accessed 10 February 2018.

xxxviii Ibid.

xxxix "Northern Expedition". *Encyclopædia Britannica.* https://www.britannica.com/event/Northern-Expedition. Accessed 10 February 2018.

xl Mao, Zedong. *Selected Works of Mao Tse-Tung: Volume 1.* 1965.

xli "People's Liberation Army". *Encyclopædia Britannica.* https://www.britannica.com/topic/Peoples-Liberation-Army-Chinese-army. Accessed 10 February 2018.

xlii Chang, Jung and Halliday, Jon. *Mao: The Unknown Story.* 2005.

xliii "Jiangxi Soviet". *Encyclopædia Britannica.* https://www.britannica.com/topic/Jiangxi-Soviet. Accessed 10 February 2018.

xliv Mao, Zedong. "Respectfully Quoted: A Dictionary of Quotations." *Bartleby.* http://www.bartleby.com/73/1933.html. Accessed 10 February 2018.

xlv "Mukden Incident". *Encyclopædia Britannica.* https://www.britannica.com/event/Mukden-Incident. Accessed 10 February 2018.

xlvi "Long March". *Encyclopædia Britannica.* https://www.britannica.com/event/Long-March. Accessed 10 February 2018.

xlvii Ibid.

xlviii Lau, Mimi. "The Long March: What it was and why it Matters to China's Xi Jinping." *South China Morning Post.* October 2016. http://www.scmp.com/news/china/policies-politics/article/2039033/long-march-what-it-was-and-why-it-matters. Accessed 10 February 2018.

xlix "Establishment of the People's Republic". *Encyclopædia Britannica*. https://www.britannica.com/place/China/Establishment-of-the-Peoples-Republic. Accessed 10 February 2018.

l "Reconstruction and Consolidation, 1949–52". *Encyclopædia Britannica*. https://www.britannica.com/place/China/Reconstruction-and-consolidation-1949-52. Accessed 10 February 2018.

li "Korean War." *Encyclopædia Britannica*. https://www.britannica.com/event/Korean-War. Accessed 10 February 2018.

lii "First Five-Year Plan." *Encyclopædia Britannica*. https://www.britannica.com/topic/First-Five-Year-Plan-Chinese-economics. Accessed 10 February 2018.

liii "Hundred Flowers Campaign." *Encyclopædia Britannica*. https://www.britannica.com/event/Hundred-Flowers-Campaign. Accessed 10 February 2018.

liv "Commune." *Encyclopædia Britannica*. https://www.britannica.com/topic/commune-Chinese-agriculture. Accessed 10 February 2018.

lv "Great Leap Forward." *Encyclopædia Britannica*. https://www.britannica.com/event/Great-Leap-Forward. Accessed 10 February 2018.

lvi Dikötter, Frank. "Mao's Great Leap to Famine." *The New York Times*. December 2010. http://www.nytimes.com/2010/12/16/opinion/16iht-eddikotter16.html?mtrref=undefined&gwh=B68D2BA84DBA7794C6E54CBC9EB5EC30&gwt=pay&assetType=opinion. Accessed 10 February 2018.

lvii Ibid.

lviii "Hai Rui Dismissed From Office." *Encyclopædia Britannica*. https://www.britannica.com/topic/Gang-of-Four#ref213744. Accessed 10 February 2018.

lix "Peng Dehuai." *Encyclopædia Britannica*. https://www.britannica.com/biography/Peng-Dehuai. Accessed 10 February 2018.

lx "Gang of Four." *Encyclopædia Britannica*. https://www.britannica.com/topic/Hai-Rui-Dismissed-From-Office. Accessed 10 February 2018.

lxi "Cultural Revolution." *Encyclopædia Britannica*. https://www.britannica.com/event/Cultural-Revolution. Accessed 10 February 2018.

lxii "Liu Shaoqi." *Encyclopædia Britannica*. https://www.britannica.com/biography/Liu-Shaoqi. Accessed 10 February 2018.

[lxiii] Phillips, Tom. "The Cultural Revolution: All You Need to Know about China's Political Convulsion." *The Guardian.* May 2016. https://www.theguardian.com/world/2016/may/11/the-cultural-revolution-50-years-on-all-you-need-to-know-about-chinas-political-convulsion. Accessed 10 February 2018.

[lxiv] Oakley, Barbara. *Evil Genes: Why Rome Fell, Hitler Rose, Enron Failed, and My Sister Stole My Mother's Boyfriend.* 2007.

[lxv] "Red Guards." *Encyclopædia Britannica.* https://www.britannica.com/topic/Red-Guards. Accessed 10 February 2018.

[lxvi] Ramzy, Austin. "China's Cultural Revolution, Explained". *The New York Times.* May 2016. https://www.nytimes.com/2016/05/15/world/asia/china-cultural-revolution-explainer.html?module=Slide&region=SlideShowTopBar&version=SlideCard-8&action=Click&contentCollection=Asia%20Pacific&slideshowTitle=Mao%E2%80%99s%20Cultural%20Revolution&currentSlide=8&entrySlide=1&pgtype=imageslideshow. Accessed 10 February 2018.

[lxvii] Mao, Yu Run. "Music under Mao, Its Background and Aftermath". *Asian Music.* 1991.

[lxviii] "Consequences of the Cultural Revolution." *Encyclopædia Britannica.* https://www.britannica.com/place/China/Consequences-of-the-Cultural-Revolution#ref71860. Accessed 10 February 2018.

[lxix] "Jiang Qing." *Encyclopædia Britannica.* https://www.britannica.com/biography/Jiang-Qing. Accessed 10 February 2018.

[lxx] Phillips, Tom. "The Cultural Revolution: All You Need to Know about China's Political Convulsion." *The Guardian.* May 2016. https://www.theguardian.com/world/2016/may/11/the-cultural-revolution-50-years-on-all-you-need-to-know-about-chinas-political-convulsion. Accessed 10 February 2018.

[lxxi] Ibid.

[lxxii] Koerner, Brendan. "What's a Maoist, Anyway?" *Slate.* February 2004. http://www.slate.com/articles/news_and_politics/explainer/2004/02/whats_a_maoist_anyway.html. Accessed 10 February 2018.

[lxxiii] Bernstein, Richard. "The Tyrant Mao, as Told by His Doctor". October 1994. *The New York Times.* http://www.nytimes.com/1994/10/02/world/the-tyrant-mao-as-told-by-his-doctor.html?pagewanted=all. Accessed 10 February 2018.

[lxxiv] Phillips, Tom. "In China Women 'Hold Up Half the Sky' but Can't Touch the Political Glass Ceiling." *The Guardian.* Oct 2017. https://www.theguardian.com/world/2017/oct/14/in-china-women-hold-up-half-the-sky-but-cant-touch-the-political-glass-ceiling. Accessed 10 February 2018.

[lxxv] Gao, Helen. "How Did Women Fare in China's Communist Revolution?" *The New York Times.* Sep 2017. https://www.nytimes.com/2017/09/25/opinion/women-china-communist-revolution.html?smid=tw-nytopinion&smtyp=cur&mtrref=www.theguardian.com&assetType=opinion. Accessed 10 February 2018.

[lxxvi] Bo, Zhiyue. "Mao Zedong: Savior or Demon?". *The Diplomat.* December 2015. https://thediplomat.com/2015/12/mao-zedong-savior-or-demon/. Accessed 10 February 2018.

Free Bonus from Captivating History (Available for a Limited time)

Hi History Lovers!

Now you have a chance to join our exclusive history list so you can get your first history ebook for free as well as discounts and a potential to get more history books for free! Simply visit the link below to join.

Captivatinghistory.com/ebook

Also, make sure to follow us on:
Twitter: @Captivhistory
Facebook: Captivating History:@captivatinghistory and Youtube: Captivating History.

ABOUT CAPTIVATING HISTORY

A lot of history books just contain dry facts that will eventually bore the reader. That's why Captivating History was created. Now you can enjoy history books that will mesmerize you. But be careful though, hours can fly by, and before you know it; you're up reading way past bedtime.

Get your first history book for free here:
http://www.captivatinghistory.com/ebook

Make sure to follow us on Twitter: @CaptivHistory and Facebook: www.facebook.com/captivatinghistory and Youtube Captivating History, so you can get all of our updates!

Made in the USA
Middletown, DE
30 March 2019